San Francisco's Cable Cars

Riding the Rope Through Past and Present

At the turn of the century in San Francisco, cable cars carried passengers in every direction.

San Francisco's Cable Cars

Riding the Rope Through Past and Present

Joyce Jansen

Foreword by Senator Dianne Feinstein
Preface by Charlotte Mailliard Swig

Woodford Press
San Francisco

Photograph Credits

Fine Arts Museums of San Francisco: Pages 11, 66-bottom, 67-top.
California Historical Society: Pages 12, 52.
San Francisco Maritime National Historic Park: Page 13.
Museum of the City of San Francisco: Pages 14, 15, 16, 17-top, 20, 23, 27, 33, 34-35, 39, 51-top, 56, 63, 67-bottom, 69, 72, 73, 75, 76, 77, 78, 79, 80, 81, 135, 136.
David Lilienstein: Front Cover, Back Cover-bottom, Page 19.
Southern Pacific Railroad Photo Archives: Pages 21, 31, 36, 45, 47-top left, 58, 59, 62-left, 64-top, 86, 87.
College of Notre Dame: Page 22.
Sheraton-Palace Hotel: Page 24, 25, 28.
Evelyn Curro: Back Cover-top, Page 32.
Pacific Coast Chapter, Railway and Locomotive Historical Society: Front Inside Cover, Back Inside Cover, Pages 6, 8, 32.
Historic Image: Pages 42-43.
San Francisco Convention & Visitors Bureau: Pages 44-top right, 105, 137, 138, 140.
Stanford News Service: Page 47-top right.
City and County of San Francisco: Pages 48, 50, 51-bottom, 71.
State of California, Sutro Library: Pages 57, 66-top.
Christopher Melching Collection: Pages 60, 62-right, 64-bottom, 84-85, 121, 122, 126-right.
The Cliff House: Pages 65, 68.
San Francisco Department of Public Transportation Photo Division: Page 83.
San Francisco Chronicle: Pages 88, 90, 93, 94.
San Francisco Public Utilities Commission: Pages 98, 99, 101, 102, 104, 108, 110, 111, 112, 119, 123.
Herbert Wicks Studios: Page 107.
John DeGroot: Page 115.
Cable Car Museum: Pages 125, 126-left, 127.
Historic American Engineering Record, Heritage Conservation & Recreation Service, Scott Dolph, 1981: Pages 128-129.
Historic American Engineering Record, Heritage Conservation & Recreation Service, H. Adams Sutphin, 1981: Pages 130, 131-bottom.
Historic American Engineering Record, Heritage Conservation & Recreation Service, M. Dombroski, 1981: Page 141-top.

Published by

Woodford Press

660 Market Street
San Francisco, California 94104

Creative Director: Laurence J. Hyman
Editor: Kate Hanley
Designer: Jim Santore

ISBN: 0-942627-12-1
Library of Congress Card Catalog Number: 95-60137

Printed in the United States of America

Contents

My warmest thanks to Dr. Albert Shumate, Joan Quigley, and Victoria Carlyle Wieland for being so supportive and helpful; to the Cable Car Museum's curator, Christopher Melching, and archivist, Emiliano Echeverria for their diligent research; and to many area museums, particularly the California Historical Society and the Bancroft Library of U. C.-Berkeley, for their resources.

Clay Street Hill Dummy and Car

1873 A HORSE CAR, DRAWN BY THE WORLD'S FIRST STREET RAILWAY CABLE CAR. 1891

"The proposition to haul a car by a rope was a simple one, and, underground in the mines, had already been demonstrated. I was unaware that anyone had attempted to use an underground traveling rope in the streets of a city for this purpose, and I felt with the light that I then possessed that the proposition was a bold one."
—Andrew Smith Hallidie

Foreword

No other city is so identified with a mode of transportation as is San Francisco with its cable cars. They are a vital part of the fabric of life in the City and a symbol of the unique combination of inventiveness and charm that mark its character.

The story of the cable car is an inextricable part of the story of San Francisco. It is a story of growth and change, of colorful characters and quirks of fate, of greed and political intrigue. But mostly it is a story of vision, industriousness, and pride of place.

The cable cars connect the San Francisco of today with the San Francisco of days gone by. Simply put, without the cable car San Francisco would not be the city it is today. In their heyday, cable cars provided access to sparsely developed outlying areas and conquered the famous hilltops. In the process, they opened up residential and business opportunities, connected neighborhoods, and influenced the work and recreation habits of all San Franciscans.

It was my pleasure to have been mayor during the cable car system's much-needed rehabilitation from 1982-1984. I was amazed by the energy our citizenry generated upon hearing that our own "Toonerville Trolley" was in dire need of costly repair. The cable cars are one issue that can unite our wonderfully diverse population.

Today San Francisco's cable car is the nation's only mobile national landmark. It is also an unmistakable expression of the spirit of a city that knows that life requires not only utility but also style. Or as *San Francisco Chronicle* columnist Herb Caen (himself something of a San Francisco institution) has written, "What other mode of public transportation brings smiles to the faces of those who have to ride in it?"

—Senator Dianne Feinstein
June 1995

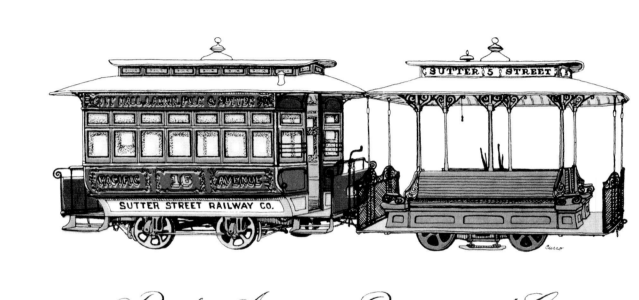

Pacific Avenue Dummy and Car

1888 THIS LINE SURVIVED THE EARTHQUAKE AND FIRE OF 1906. 1929

Preface

When it comes to our cable cars, San Franciscans maintain a great deal of pride. I had the honor and pleasure of experiencing the enthusiasm this town generates over its beloved hill climbers—while working to organize celebrations for the cars' centennial in 1973, their rehabilitation in 1982, and their comeback in 1984—and it was overwhelming indeed.

During the two years when the cable cars were absent from our streets, it seemed as though San Francisco's magic had faded. Only then did we realize how much the sounds of cables whirring, bells ringing, and gripmen shouting added to the City's atmosphere.

We San Franciscans gladly share our cable cars with scores of visitors each year. Now, thanks to Joyce Jansen's dedication and diligence, we can also offer the fascinating history of how the cable cars came to be a San Francisco trademark. Her work captures the elusive and enchanting spirit of the cable cars and, in doing so, the City they serve so well.

—Charlotte Mailliard Swig
June 1995

Hub of the Wild West

A s they waited to cross the street on a damp, windy San Francisco day in 1869, thirty-three-year-old Andrew Hallidie and his friend, Joe Britton, watched in horror as a passenger-carrying horse car struggling up Jackson Street encountered trouble. One horse slipped on the wet cobblestones, causing the other horses, unable to escape their rigging, to fall and be dragged down the street. The passengers were unharmed, but all the horses suffered broken legs and had to be destroyed.

Knowing of Hallidie's mechanical abilities and interests, Britton turned to Hallidie—an engineer, bridge-builder, and one-time miner—and said,

In 1849, San Francisco was a pristine oasis. This is the future site of Golden Gate Park.

"Andrew, why don't you put that wire rope of yours to use pulling these cars and prevent these accidents?"

This scene would replay often in Hallidie's mind as he developed his plans to provide San Francisco with the first-known form of mass transportation to navigate hills safely. In time Hallidie's efforts would spawn an invention that would revolutionize public transportation, signify all that is unique about San Francisco, and capture the imagination of people around the world: the cable car.

Born in Dumfries, Scotland on

March 16, 1836, Andrew Hallidie Smith was named after his father ("Andrew"), and his uncle and godfather ("Hallidie"), who was a physician to King William IV and Queen Victoria. Years later, Andrew would legally change his name to Andrew Smith Hallidie, as he felt his adopted home of San Francisco was overcrowded with Smiths.

Early in Hallidie's life, his family moved to London, where his mother died in 1845. As a child, Hallidie was fascinated by things mechanical and scientific. Impatient with the process of a formal education, he often read technical books at night. At thirteen, he began working in his older brother's machine shop. Three years later, Hallidie and his father decided to travel to Northern California to investigate a gold mine in Mariposa County.

In January 1852, father and son set sail from Liverpool aboard the *Pacific*. The ship carried fifty passengers, and those who had already been to California invited the eager youngster into their conversation as they told outrageous tales of the "Wild West," a region populated by thugs and thieves hungry for gold. En route, the Smiths stayed briefly at New York's Astor Hotel. From New York they sailed aboard the *Brother Jonathan* to the Isthmus of Panama, where they boarded the *Brutus*. After a total of fifty-nine days in transit, the Smiths landed in San Francisco on May 24 at Clark's Point, at the foot of Telegraph Hill at Broadway. There they saw a clutter of ships in the harbor; nearly five hundred square riggers, schooners, and barges had been abandoned in the mud alongside crudely built boardwalks leading to the shore. More ships teeming with immigrants were arriving on an average of seven per day. Newcomers were also arriving via the perilous overland route. In just a few short years, this remote western outpost had been transformed into a hub of frenzied activity.

The Spanish had officially established Mission Dolores on June 29, 1776. They also set up a stronghold, known as the Presidio, on the edge of the Golden Gate. The land around the hamlet of Yerba Buena, as the City was known until 1847, was dominated by rolling sand dunes sweeping around hills of bedrock. There were few settlers. Seeking to establish a bastion at the western edge of the continent, the United States Army assumed control of the Presidio in 1847.

On January 24, 1848, everything began to change dramatically.

In the Sierra Nevada foothills along the South Fork of the American River, about 140 miles northeast of San Francisco, Johann Augustus Sutter operated a saw mill. His foreman, James Marshall, was making a routine inspection when something shimmering in the sawmill's tailrace caught his eye. Kneeling down, Marshall picked up a golden nugget. He asked the camp housekeeper, Elizabeth Wimmer, to drop the nugget in the kettle of lye she was boiling to make soap. After the nugget had boiled all day without tarnishing, Marshall knew he had found gold.

Sutter hoped to keep Marshall's discovery a secret, fearing his employees would bolt to seek their own fortunes. Sam Brannan, an early Mormon settler who ran a general store near the mill, also hoped to suppress the story until he could stock his store well enough to outfit the anticipated onslaught

Andrew Smith Hallidie

*The view from Rincon Hill, one of the City's first prestigious residential areas,
in 1851. Many boats were abandoned in the harbor by those eager to go after
the gold.*

North Beach, 1856

Yerba Buena, spring 1837

of miners. But one trip to an assayer launched news of the gold. The skippers of ships hauling lumber from the river to points all along the Pacific Coast quickly spread the news that gold had been discovered in the hills near San Francisco, which they called "the City."

Sutter, it turned out, did lose his crew and he eventually died broke.

By 1849, people from everywhere in the world were pouring into Northern California, and San Francisco's growth was unabated. In 1850, San Francisco was officially chartered as a city and California gained statehood on September 9. As the population boomed, scores of wooden shacks cropped up among the hills of San Francisco that rose as high as 925 feet. These now-renowned hills are known today as Telegraph Hill, Nob Hill, Russian Hill, Potrero Hill, and so forth. Streets were constructed hastily to accommodate the influx of new residents, and were lined with cobblestones or flimsy wooden planks that became treacherous in the frequent fog and rain. The growing population, coupled with San Francisco's unique physiography and climate, demanded forms of transportation that could haul freight and people up treacherous inclines.

From 1849 to 1851, this bustling new community, built mostly of wood, was leveled by fire at least six times. The fires lent San Francisco an eerie, desolate air. Few houses survived the flames, and residents often camped in tents on Telegraph Hill. The City was constantly reinventing itself, rebuilding almost as quickly as it was destroyed, and piles of lumber on the

VIEW OF
SAN FRANCISCO.
1850.
Taken from a high point on the south side.
Published by the Author of "Sights in the Gold Region &c".

San Francisco, 1850

street were commonplace. The continual arrival of ships laden with goods allowed the storekeepers swiftly to restock their shelves with everything needed to fuel the reconstruction, including—as befit a wild, raucous new town—lots of liquor.

By 1853, San Francisco had approximately fifty-thousand citizens. Many new residents came from the South, either with the military or to escape building political pressures, and one could often hear reverent choruses of such songs as "My Old Kentucky Home." The City was characterized by ethnic diversity, with large communities of Spanish, Mexican, French, German, Indian, and Italian immigrants. Later, many Chinese were imported to provide cheap labor.

The female population slowly increased as women came to San Francisco to meet up with the men they had known at home. As early as 1853, Mrs.

San Francisco in 1849, on the verge of mass expansion.

*David Scannell, fire chief during the
"Silver Seventies," was one of the riders
on the first-ever cable car trip.*

A. B. Easton recognized the problem of stranded women who followed husbands or lovers to the coast and then were unable to locate them. Many resorted to supporting themselves as prostitutes. In order to provide shelter for these women, Mrs. Easton founded the Ladies Protection and Relief Society.

As women and money became more prevalent, the steamers carrying goods to San Francisco began to haul items of a more fashionable nature. Kid boots and gloves in vivid colors were imported from France and elaborate silks were brought in from Asia. These wares were sold at dry goods emporiums such as the City of Paris. With gold as their tender, shopping occupied much of the women's time.

Many of the population then were referred to as "Sydney Ducks;" England regularly transported its criminals to a penal colony in Botany Bay, Australia, and when news of the Gold Rush reached Australia, prisoners were released to seek their fortunes in California. Their presence enhanced San Francisco's reputation of lawlessness, which grew despite the formation of the Committee of Vigilance to control and discourage crime.

The miners were another colorful—if not necessarily tasteful—segment of society. They arrived from the gold fields unshaven and haggard, dressed in high boots, flannel shirts, riveted jeans, and floppy hats. After bathing and dressing up, the miners spent much of their time in San Francisco gambling and drinking.

The elder Smith decided after a year in California that this ruggedness was not for him, and he returned to London. Andrew bade his father goodbye and headed for the mines in the mountains.

Wire Ropes, Railroads, Silver Mines, and a Free Lunch

L ife in the gold country was rough. Miners had to contend with bandits, thieves, Native Americans who resisted their arrival, and inclement winter weather. Hallidie enjoyed the company of other prospectors but did not indulge in their bouts of drinking and gambling. Instead he busied himself learning mining techniques and fostering his already well-developed technical talents: He repaired old guns, a talent he had learned in London, pounded out makeshift tools for the miners, surveyed roads, and investigated potential waterways.

Perhaps Hallidie's greatest achievement at the time was his perfection of a product that his father had patented in England: wire rope. His father had sold this invention to the shipping and mining industries in England,

The versatile and sturdy wire rope.

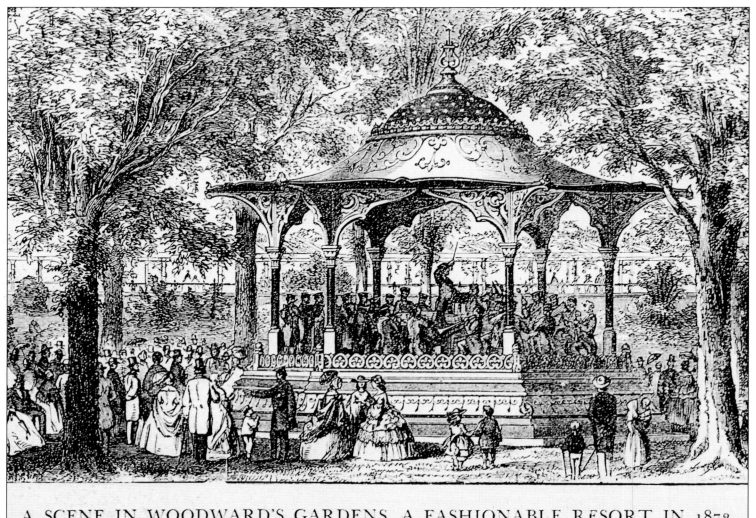

A SCENE IN WOODWARD'S GARDENS, A FASHIONABLE RESORT IN 1873

where it was used in ship riggings and in underground railways in coal mines. Hallidie introduced the rope to the Pacific Coast in 1856 and put it to use hauling ore and workers out of the mines.

The rope's main achievement was its ability to bend—as over a pulley—and straighten out while maintaining considerable strength. Hallidie's cable had a tensile strength of 160,000 pounds per square inch, yet was only 1.25 inches wide. Nineteen strands of crucible steel wire gave the cable its strength, while a core of hemp provided its flexibility.

During the five years he lived in the gold country, from 1852 to 1857, the young Scotsman faced continual adventure and challenge. In 1855, at the age of nineteen, Hallidie overcame many natural hazards and completed a suspension bridge and aqueduct across the Middle Fork of the American

Above, Henry Casebolt's "Balloon Car," a horse-drawn predecessor to the cable car so-named for its unusual oval-shaped roof. At the end of the line, these cars rotated on a pivot to face the opposite direction. The pivots frequently wore out, resulting in an uneasy ride. The line offered service to Woodward's Gardens, opposite, an elaborate amusement park located at Mission and Fourteenth streets.

River at Horse Shoe Bar. The bridge spanned nearly two hundred feet and was used to transport water to the miners.

During this time Andrew made several trips to San Francisco via Wells Fargo Stage Coach, but he always returned to the mines of the Mother Lode to pan for gold in Calaveras, Amador, El Dorado, Placer, and Nevada counties. He and his fellow prospectors were so intent on finding gold they failed to realize that in nearby Nevada the dark blue clay contained enough silver ore to dwarf the riches of the Gold Rush. The mines in Nevada came to be known as the Washoe, after a local Indian tribe, and Comstock Lode, after Henry T. Comstock, who held first claim.

Finally accepting that his picks and pans had failed him, Hallidie moved to San Francisco in 1857. He continued producing wire rope, and con-

William Chapman Ralston was widely hailed as "The Man Who Built San Francisco."

OCCIDENTAL HOTEL.
OPENED TO PUBLIC
JAN. 1. 1863.

#373
T. E. HECHT

Many early San Franciscans lived in plush residential hotels such as the Occidental. The City of Paris, located at street level, sold elegant fashions from all over the world.

structed suspension bridges across the Klamath River and the American River at Nevada City, and at Folsom, California.

San Francisco was a popular destination for frustrated prospectors. The City offered them a chance to open other lucrative industries catering to those lucky enough to have tapped the wealth of the mines. Banks, hotels, shops, and bars led many to their fortunes. One man who excelled in these offshoot industries was William Chapman Ralston. Billy Ralston had been a riverboat captain in Plymouth, Ohio when he met Joseph Donohoe and Eugene Kelly. These men told tales of abundant wealth in San Francisco, where they hoped to open a new bank, and invited Ralston to visit them there. When he arrived, Donohoe and Kelly asked him to be a partner in their bank, but Ralston decided instead to found his own bank with a new partner, Sacramento financier Darius Ogden Mills. On July 5, 1864, Ralston opened the Bank of California.

Ralston envisioned San Francisco as a world-class city, and as cashier of the Bank of California, he had the resources to implement his dreams. In 1869, he retained architect Samuel C. Bugbee to design the California Theater on Bush Street. Ralston hired actors Lawrence Barrett and John McCullogh to oversee the theater, and their first production was aptly titled *Money*. Ralston also founded the Mission Woolen Mills, Pacific Sugar Refinery, Kimball Carriage Factory, West Coast Furniture Manufacturing,

Ralston's plans for his elegant Palace Hotel, top, detailed a stunning interior courtyard. Below, Andrew Hallidie's California Wire Works had its main factory in the heart of North Beach.

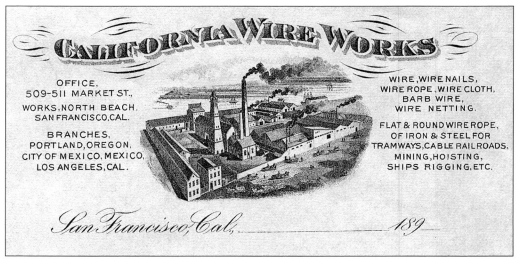

The Oriental Hotel was one of early San Francisco's finest hotels. This scene, from 1853, shows actress Lola Montez and Sam Brannan seated in the carriage.

and teamed with Agoston Haraszathy to form the Sonoma County Vinicultural Society.

In the wake of wealth and enterprise, many San Francisco residents soon became accustomed to luxury. While some built elaborate homes, many others found the lush accommodations and cooking and cleaning services of residential hotels such as the Occidental, the Oriental, the Grand, and Lick House more to their liking. Permanent lodgers often furnished their apartments with fine French furniture, crystal, silver services, and famous paintings. James Lick, a former Pennsylvanian who made his fortune in trade and real estate in South America, built his inn with an elegant dining room complete with mahogany and teak paneling and numerous works of art.

Francois L. A. Pioche, a banker from France who moved to San Francisco in 1847, imported forty chefs from Paris to produce the native cuisine he so missed. He found employment for them in various hotels and such restaurants as the Poodle Dog, Maison Riche, and Maison Doree. These well-schooled chefs educated their customers in the art of dining and established a culinary standard for the renowned French cuisine in San Francisco today.

Some establishments, including the Lick House, What Cheer, and Russ House, generously presented free lunches consisting of an array of meats and cheeses, ham in champagne sauce, and fresh salmon. Prized buffets included terrapin—the giant sea turtle—artfully served in its shell. The sumptuous food was accompanied by equally extravagant drink. Saloons imported ice from Alaska to chill their champagne, particularly popular because women were not allowed to have mixed drinks. It was served straight up, mixed into a punch, or as "Black Velvet," a glass of champagne with a float of stout. Miners frequented the Auction Lunch Saloon, run by James Flood and Billy O'Brien, located adjacent to the Mining Exchange. Mining tips could frequently be gleaned from overheard conversations.

Flood and O'Brien had a stake in the Comstock, along with partners Jim Fair and John Mackay. Fair and Mackay had a genuine nose for ore and lived in Virginia City, the hub of Nevada's silver mining activities. These four men would come to be known as the "Irish Quartet of Bonanza Kings" because of their later persistence and good fortune in investing in the Consolidated Virginia Mines, which went into bonanza. John Mackay enjoyed such good fortune that he ordered a fifteen hundred-piece silver service from Tiffany's to be made for his wife, Louise, with Consolidated Virginia silver that he had mined himself.

In 1864, Ralston hoped to profit from the Comstock by opening a branch of his bank in Virginia City. William Sharon heard of Ralston's plan and entreated Ralston to trust him with the responsibility of running the Virginia City branch. Although Sharon had no prior banking experience, Ralston respected Sharon's reputation as an astute poker player and gave him the job. In his new position Sharon freely loaned money to miners, and, if they were late on their payments, he foreclosed on the loans and seized the miners' claims. He and Ralston formed the Union Mill and Mining Company, and ultimately made millions from the Comstock.

The Comstock mines were located on a two-mile fissure and were worked twenty-four hours a day, with deposits bringing up to thirty dollars per ounce. Writers such as Bret Harte, in his *Overland Monthly*, and Mark Twain, a contributor to the *Virginia City Territorial Enterprise*, wrote of the great Comstock and Washoe strikes, where it seemed any day someone might strike it rich. And Andrew Hallidie's wire rope was hauling the silver out of most of these mines.

In order to address the needs of the mining industry, Hallidie gave up building bridges. He started buying shiploads of old horseshoes and converting them into wire rope at his own factory, first named the A. S. Hallidie Company but later changed to California Wire Works. Thanks to the impetus provided by the Comstock Lode, the company employed more than two hundred men.

In the fall of 1863, Hallidie married Martha Elizabeth Woods. Born in Quincy, Illinois on June 6, 1846, "Mattie" had moved to Sacramento with her father, David Woods, a fine cabinet maker. There the bright and charming Mattie met and married the industrious Andrew.

The Mechanics' Institute in 1865, located on Union Square at the corner of Geary and Stockton streets.

While Hallidie had been away mining, San Francisco had slowly moved away from its earlier incarnation as a rugged and roguish town. By 1856, thirteen daily newspapers existed, and there were weeklies in several languages. In 1864, Andrew sought to encourage interest in reading among the rowdy population by establishing free public libraries. His civic-minded friends Joe Britton, Henry Davis, and Jim Moffitt agreed to help.

James Lick, who was earning a fortune in real estate in addition to his income from the Lick House, contributed $450,000. With this final piece of assistance, the Mechanics' Institute was opened, temporarily housed in a building owned by Sam Brannan until a permanent home could be built. The purpose of the institute was to establish a library, a reading room, and a cabinet of scientific apparati, and to house works of art. In 1864, Hallidie was named the Institute's president.

Hallidie also promoted scholarly pursuits as a regent for the College of California, which had been founded in Oakland in 1855. In 1868, Andrew teamed with Rev. Horatio Stebbins, Samuel Butterworth, and Billy Ralston to rename the college the University of California and move it to 160 acres of beautifully wooded hills along Strawberry Creek in Berkeley. As president of the Mechanics' Institute, Andrew was an ex officio member of the board of regents of the University. He had the unique role of holding the office of regent as both an appointed and an ex officio member. At a banquet hosted by the board of architects, Hallidie outlined his hopes "that this

The original Palace Hotel opened in 1875. Carriages entered this handsome courtyard from New Montgomery Street.

great university be free, absolutely free, and open alike to men and women to produce refined, fresh minds."

In 1869, San Francisco was linked with the rest of the continent. Obsessed with the possibilities of a transcontinental railroad, Theodore Judah, an engineer who had arrived in Sacramento in 1854, spent years surveying the region yet to be crossed by train tracks and lobbying in Washington for a California railroad. He enlisted Collis P. Huntington and Mark Hopkins, who were partners in a hardware store; Leland Stanford, a grocer; and Charles Crocker, a former blacksmith, to back his venture.

Huntington, Hopkins, Stanford, and Crocker contributed $1,500 each so that Judah could undertake the building of his proposed Central Pacific Railroad. Construction began in January 1863, and Judah headed for New York hoping to raise enough money to buy out his partners. While crossing the Isthmus of Panama, he contracted yellow fever and died.

The official linking of the Union Pacific Railroad with the Central Pacific Railroad was achieved when Stanford drove a "gold" spike into the ground at Promontory, Utah on May 10, 1869. Stanford was installed as president of the Central Pacific Railroad, and he and his partners moved into history as "the Big Four."

Recognizing that the transcontinental railroad would bring droves of visitors to San Francisco gave further fuel to Billy Ralston's ambitions to raise his beloved city's stature as an international cosmopolitan center. He wanted to do away with the wooden shacks and look of flimsiness that had characterized the City in its early days and replace them with elegance worthy of a world-class city. With help from William Sharon, now a senator from Nevada, Ralston raised $5 million. In 1875, Ralston started construction of his dream: a lavish hotel to be named the Palace.

Ralston planned a seven-story building, with eight hundred guest rooms, to be built at the corner of Montgomery and Market streets. Luxury and elegance were the watchwords, and no expense was to be spared in their pursuit.

Ralston imported white marble from Vermont, black marble from Tennessee, linen from Ireland, and Haviland china from France. He used California oak planking for floors, California laurel for furniture, and Mexican primavera and South American mahogany throughout the building. New York's W. & J. Sloane & Co., secured the carpeting contract, using a great deal of specially woven Axminister. Gorham silver was monogrammed with "Palace Hotel," undoubtedly tempting souvenir collectors. Ralston ordered the best available construction materials to make the structure as earthquake-proof as possible. There were even four artesian wells beneath the hotel to serve the hotel's daily needs and for use in firefighting.

A carriage entrance off New Montgomery Street led through a massive archway lit by huge gas lanterns into a glass-domed inner court. Each of the seven stories had balconies to enable guests to look down onto the court.

During the construction of the Palace, Ralston's generosity and overzealous ambitions for San Francisco began to backfire. His businesses were failing because of eastern competition that resulted from the transcontinental railway. His mines were operating with heavy losses because of several casualties in the Yellow Jacket Mine. A sudden drain on the Bank of California spurred Ralston to borrow $750,000 from his partner Darius Mills. He was overextended in every direction. Ralston's only hope for a source of income was the sale of his latest pet project, the Spring Valley Water Company, to the City. *The Bulletin* and *The Call* were thwarting his efforts with unflattering portraits of his craftiness.

Desperate for cash, Ralston reportedly offered his prized Palace Hotel for $1.7 million to Sharon, who declined to come up with the cash. Bank president Mills and the bank's board of directors called for Ralston's resignation. Ralston understood their fears, but stalled because he was confident that Spring Valley Water Company would provide his financial salvation. To pay his debts, Ralston signed over everything he owned to Sharon in trust. The board suspended business and closed to reorganize. Depositors angrily voiced their fears they had been swindled.

Ralston resigned and went home to announce the sad news to his family. He told his wife, Lizzie, that they would have to move in with her stepfather, Colonel J. D. Fry. He returned to the bank the next morning, and, as was his custom, went swimming in the Bay that afternoon. This time he didn't return. The news quickly spread through town, raising considerable speculation regarding the circumstances of his death. At age forty-nine, Ralston had been in fair health and was an excellent swimmer. The coroner's report announced the official cause of death as a stroke, and Lizzie was paid $65,000 from his insurance policy. In his memory, the Bank of California was draped in black.

Barely two months later, October 2, 1875, William Sharon opened the Palace Hotel. Crowds hurried in to view the spectacle, which was designed by John P. Gaynor. The hotel formally opened on October 14 with a three-and-a-half-hour dinner prepared by Chef de Cuisine Jules Harder in honor of General Phillip Sheridan, a hero in the Franco-Prussian War.

The Bank of California also reopened on October 2, but San Franciscans continued to grieve over Ralston, "the man who built San Francisco," albeit with Nevada's silver.

Upon Ralston's death, Sharon lost no time in overtaking Ralston's estate in Belmont, twenty-two miles south of San Francisco. Many people were unhappy with the settlements they received from Sharon for Ralston's debts, and he was sued often. Mrs. Ralston was among those who brought suit, but she made an out-of-court settlement of $250,000, a mere pittance since she had four children to support and Ralston's properties had been worth millions.

Sharon had proven himself a man of questionable ethics with his unmerciful loan policies in Virginia City. He continued his ways in San Francisco, where he kept a mistress, Sarah Althea Hill, at the Grand Hotel and reportedly paid her $500 a month. Perhaps his most malicious turn had come when he tried, unsuccessfully, to spread a rumor that Ralston had consumed poison before drowning.

William Sharon died in 1885 at the age of sixty-five. Commenting in an epitaph, business and civic leader Adolph Sutro said: "That man is dead—I would not like to say much about him. I think Sharon was a thoroughly bad man—a man entirely void of principle, honesty, and gentility."

Hallidie's Folly

The vigorous growth of early San Francisco gave rise to logistical matters that demanded attention. San Franciscans met in the many saloons not only to imbibe but also to conduct business and discuss the needs of the City. Often when an idea was developed, the concerned parties would head for City Hall to obtain a franchise from the Board of Supervisors, securing the rights for their idea no matter how loosely formulated it might be.

By 1869, public transportation needs still had not been met adequately. The first form of mass conveyance appeared in 1852—the Omnibus Railroad Company, a horse-drawn bus service popularly known as the Yellow Line because of the color of its cars. The original line ran from the post office at Clay and Kearny streets to Mission Dolores. By 1857, the Yellow Line covered several routes, and the fare was ten cents. The horses, which wore strands of bells to alert pedestrians of their approach, could only work an hour or so before requiring lengthy rest. Because of frequent accidents and overwork the average life of a horse was only four-and-a-half years. These "hay-burners" also presented the perpetual problem of streets full of droppings.

A serene Market Street (at Post) in 1876, before cable cars dominated the thoroughfare.

The Steam Dummy and Car
A NOISY NON-HILL-CLIMBING CONTEMPORARY OF THE CABLE CAR.

Steam cars were not only inefficient but also unpopular. Their noisy, flame-belching engines scared passengers.

John McLaren, later supervisor of Golden Gate Park, once relieved some of this problem by accepting ten thousand pounds of horse manure, to be used as park fertilizer, as a birthday present from the Board of Supervisors.

Advancing technology introduced steam cars in 1860, but the horse cars remained more popular. So much fuel was required to power the steam cars in the stop-and-start city traffic that the cars spewed flames, frightening passengers. Fares were fifty cents daily and one dollar on weekends. Steam cars were only feasible for long, flat journeys, such as that between San Francisco and San Jose. But neither of these transportation options could conquer San Francisco's imposing hills. The City desperately needed an inexpensive, effective means of public transportation that would also make land more accessible for real estate developments.

In 1869, Andrew Hallidie determined he would provide the solution. As he later wrote: "My attention was called to the great difficulty experienced in hauling the street cars up one of the steep streets of San Francisco, and the great cruelty and hardship to the horses engaged in that work. I devoted all my available time to the careful consideration of the subject." The following year he set out, with great foresight and deliberation, to create a cable car system that would run along a continuous cable powered by a steam generator. Hallidie had effectively employed similar systems for hauling in mines, but the idea was untried as a form of urban transportation.

Realizing that streets torn up to accommodate cables would have to be

This is one of Hallidie's original fleet, circa 1874. Bearded Andrew Hallidie is seated in the front row, next to Mayor A. J. Bryant. Mattie Hallidie is also seated in the front row. Hallidie's screw-clamp grip, located directly behind Mayor Bryant, would soon be replaced by a more manageable lever grip.

repaved, Hallidie first founded the California Paving Company. He then hired engineer David R. Smith to draft plans to construct a cable railway up California Street on Nob Hill, the toughest and steepest hill to surmount.

But Hallidie's idea of a cable car was not original. In 1869, the San Francisco Board of Supervisors granted C. S. Bushnell, Abner Doubleday, E. W. Steele, and Benjamin S. Brooks franchise No. 944, which provided for an extensive network of street railways. These men may have had a legal edge over Hallidie in their quest to build a cable car system, but their plans to implement the railroad were far from complete: They lacked a patent for a gripping device and an instrument of propulsion such as wire rope.

When Hallidie tried to obtain financial support, people around town doubted his ability to move cars with no visible driving force and regarded his scheme as "Hallidie's Folly." The steam cars had not been a financial

The machinery that powered the cables was truly awesome for its day. The cable system used steam generators until 1911, when electricity was instituted.

success, and there was no proof that cable cars would work, much less make a profit. This town, built on speculation, seemed to have had its fill.

In an 1890 report to the Mechanics' Institute, Hallidie detailed his struggle. He wrote, plaintively, that only his partners in the Mechanics' Institute—Britton, Davis, and Moffitt—offered any sort of encouragement. "From almost every source, doubt and skepticism were expressed."

One exception was the Society for the Prevention of Cruelty to Animals (SPCA), which was appalled by the City's reliance on horse-drawn cars. When word of Hallidie's ideas reached the SPCA, their members endorsed him publicly. Unfortunately, Hallidie's plans had to be postponed when a previous contractual commitment forced David Smith to leave for a job in Central America.

Refusing to be dismayed, Hallidie sought ways to revive his project. He

Market Street looking west toward the Grand Hotel and the Palace Hotel in 1880.

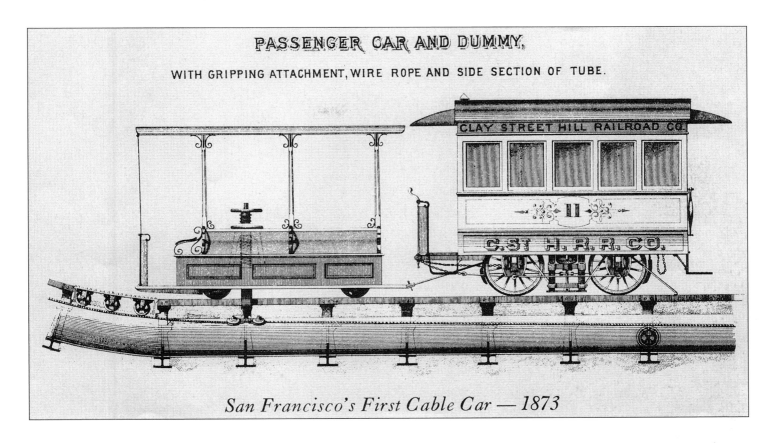

PASSENGER CAR AND DUMMY,

WITH GRIPPING ATTACHMENT, WIRE ROPE AND SIDE SECTION OF TUBE.

San Francisco's First Cable Car — 1873

decided that Clay Street would be just as effective a route as California Street, and since it was less steep he reasoned it would therefore be less costly. He hired a new draftsman, William Epplesheimer, and work on the Clay Street Hill Railroad began in 1872.

Once again, Hallidie had trouble raising financial support. "Even friendly disposed engineers shook their heads and gave wise counsel to their friends to let some others put in their money and do the experimenting," he later wrote. So Hallidie and his supporters circulated a pamphlet outlining the proposed system and produced a working model of the car, which was displayed at the Clay Street Bank. Those who owned property on the Clay Street hill were solicited for support, and ultimately they promised to pay about $40,000 once the line was complete. E. Willard Burr of the Clay Street Bank, in a rare show of business support, agreed to advance $30,000 on bonds and mortgage of the line for ten years at ten percent interest, but the public showed little interest in buying the shares.

In May, Hallidie and his partners in the Mechanics' Institute personally insured the survival of the cable car project by buying all the unsold shares of the company and advancing a final $60,000.

Now added to Hallidie's pressures was a final deadline of August 1, when "the franchise under which we worked, and which already had been extended once, would expire. It was imperative to have the engines and cables working and to make a trip over the road by that time." The franchise also required that a trip with paying passengers be made on that day.

The actual date of the first cable car run has been the source of much dispute. Although Hallidie, in his papers, names August 1 as the cutoff date, all 1873 newspaper articles that detailed the scene name August 2. As a result, August 2 has come to be known as the first day the cable cars ran.

On the morning of August 2, 1873, Hallidie feared that the brakes on the "dummy," or grip, car were not in proper working order and orchestrated a trial run at dawn. The dummy car was used to tow the passenger car because Hallidie believed that one long car would be too heavy and thus impractical on the steep grade. To test the dummy car's safety, he attached ropes to the car, tied them off on a telephone pole at the top of the Clay Street hill at Jones, and gradually lowered the car down the hill: "We found, by using care and holding on [to the levers pressing on the wheels], we could control the car, and it was hauled back to its starting place."

Finally, Hallidie was ready to prove the validity of his much-doubted cable cars in an official test run, and none too soon. In his report, he wrote:

> The morning was foggy and gray and, when ready to pick up the rope, the man who had been placed in charge of the grip showed such signs of fear that I was compelled to take his place, pick up the rope, and take the car down the hill.
>
> On the way down, we threw off the rope and picked it up repeatedly; slacked the grip, stopped the car, and ran it back, and made such experiments as opportunity offered.
>
> At the terminus at Kearny Street, the car was turned around and transferred to the up track and taken up the hill without any difficulty or delay.
>
> The operation was an earnest one. There was no frivolity. The whole affair was serious, and when it was done, there was simply a mutual handshaking, and nothing but cold water drank.
>
> People were asleep, and, with the exception of one enthusiastic Frenchman who thrust his red night-capped head out of the window as we went by on the down trip and threw us a faded bouquet, there was no demonstration.

Jimmy Hewitt, a retired locomotive engineer, was the originally-intended gripman. As he peered down the Clay Street hill behind the grip of a never-before-tested cable car, his queasy stomach and knocking knees caused him to abandon his chance to be the father of all gripmen.

Hallidie had invited Tom Burns, son of his bookkeeper, and Valentine Rey, son of Joe Britton's partner, Jacques Rey, to ride along on this maiden voyage. Jim Moffitt's eight-year-old son, James, stood at the summit of Clay and Jones streets and watched the world's first cable car come up the hill, proud of his father's contribution to this new contraption.

The all-important revenue run, a requirement of the franchise, came that

Early cable car riders referred to a trip on the cable car as "riding the rope," and donned their finest for the journey. Andrew Hallidie is operating the grip.

afternoon. A crowd of the curious, the skeptical, and the prominent gathered at Clay and Kearny streets to witness or participate in the first public ride.

Mayor William Alvord, Fire Chief David Scannell, Chief of Police Patrick Crowley, Sheriff James Adams, Supervisors Timothy McCarthy and Samuel Taylor, and nearly eighty-five other people jammed themselves on board.

An article from the *Daily Alta California*, dated August 3, 1873, reported: "An enthusiastic and ambitious young lady followed the car the distance of more than a block, begging the privilege of riding and was finally taken aboard by the sympathizing male monopolists. On entering the car, she walked up to the cash box and dropped a five-cent piece, remarking that she would always have the satisfaction of saying she was the first lady who ever rode that line of cars."

Put to a severe test, the overcrowded cable car successfully inched its way up all 307 feet of Clay Street. Hallidie and his associates breathed a great sigh of relief. The evening edition of the *San Francisco Bulletin* praised the day's event: "The success of the experiment was greater than the projectors anticipated. . . . The facility with which the fastener can be made to cling to the cable is wonderful. There is none of the jerking anticipated, owing to the gradual tightening of the clamp around the cable."

By the time the first revenue run was over, saloons all over town were crowded as toasts were raised to Hallidie. San Franciscans seldom needed an excuse to celebrate, but this day was especially significant, and people rejoiced accordingly. Duncan Nicol's Bank Exchange, located on Montgomery near Clay, was packed with celebrants drinking his trademark "Pisco punch," a secret and highly potent recipe whose main ingredient was Peruvian grape brandy. At Hallidie's favorite establishment, the Lick House, diners feasted on eastern oysters, soup Julienne, salade d'Achois, terrapin, lamb chops, sauce tartare, chicken livers a la Lyonnaise, celery, olives, filet de volaille aux truffles, asparagus, sherbet, turkey, French lettuce, ice cream, biscuit glacé, fruit, Roquefort and Stilton cheeses, and French bon-bons. Wines served included Haut Sauterne, Chateau d'Yquem, Duff Gordon sherry, claret, Roederer champagne, and plenty of cognac.

Andrew Hallidie's "folly" was a success.

Nob Hill

From its inception the cable car was joyously adopted by San Franciseans as an embodiment of individuality and resourcefulness. But the cable cars' momentum as a viable business venture was slower to build. The Clay Street Hill Railroad started providing regular service almost a month after its historic first run, and remained the City's only cable line for the next four years. Although it had proved to be an engineering marvel, the fulfillment of the cable car's practical potential required the building of additional lines.

Henry Casebolt, owner of the Sutter Street Railway, was the next to endorse cable cars when he converted his horse-drawn cars to Hallidie's underground cable system. Casebolt had experimented with overhead cables in Piedmont, a suburb of Oakland, but they were unsightly and he gained little support. After four months, Casebolt abandoned his project and opened a cable line using Hallidie's underground system on January 27, 1877. Casebolt's line extended from Market, Sutter, and Sansome streets to the power house on Larkin and Bush streets, and the fare was five cents.

The Sutter Street line and the Clay Street Railroad began to expand the use of dummy cars, which were originally intended for gripmen and instruments only. Seats were added

A California Street car glides past Mark Hopkins' palatial home at California and Mason streets in 1893. Hopkins did not live to see his mansion completed.

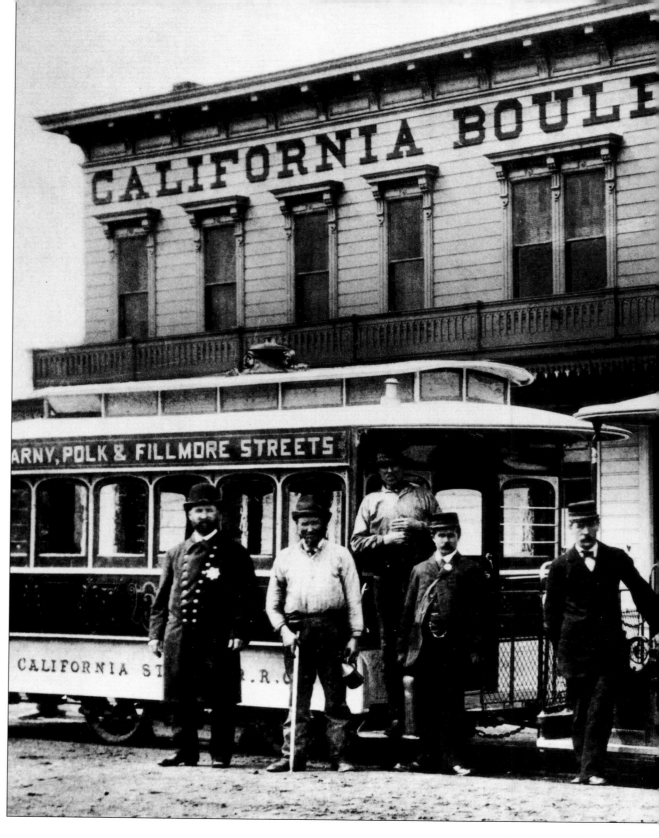

The California Street cars, designed by Henry Root, introduced the lever grip still used today. The men in blue jeans and floppy hats were probably newly-arrived from the gold mines.

Left, the fashionable Lillie Hitchcock Coit in the late 1870s after she decided she'd like to be a blonde. Above, traffic posed no problem in 1880 on the City's second cable line.

for passenger use on the sides and front, leaving the central area for the gripman and his array of wheels, levers, cranks, and pedals. Trailer cars had a seating capacity of eighteen, dummies sixteen.

The unassuming cable car slowly shaped the city it served. As new lines provided convenient access to hilltop neighborhoods, they consequently gave sudden wealth to thousands of property owners. Possibilities for development that had been unthinkable were suddenly alive as new homes were constructed and new businesses opened. Riding to visit the shops that opened along the Sutter Street line allowed fashionable ladies to show off their latest gowns. This prompted another social phenomenon to spring from cable cars: "going calling." Calling was not only a favorite pastime, it was considered one of society's requisites. If one woman called on another but was not received, a card was left with one corner turned up. If one's coachman was sent in, the card was left unturned. If a woman was popular enough to have her own reception day, she stayed in to receive visitors on whatever afternoon was hers. The latest news of stocks was exchanged along with choice bits of gossip.

Women delighted in going calling on the Sutter Street and Clay Street cable cars. Among the strong supporters of calling by cable car was the

Southern Pacific's headquarters at Fourth and Townsend in 1887. Steam trains, such as the one shown on the right, were well suited for the journey down the Peninsula, where many of San Francisco's elite had second homes.

socially prominent Lillie Hitchcock Coit, whose own reception time was Thursday afternoon. Lillie was recognized as an arbiter of fashion. If she carried a walking stick on Wednesday, by Saturday five hundred women would be seen carrying a similar cane. She was also known for being favored by the famed Volunteer Fire Department's Knickerbocker Engine No. 5, whose members had to be natives of New York. She qualified because her father, Major Charles Hitchcock, M.D., had been stationed at West Point when she was born in 1843, and the firemen made her their only female honorary member. Proud of her exclusive membership, Coit had all her Parisian lingerie embroidered "LHC5," and signed "5" after her name.

Lillie and her husband, Howard, were an extremely popular couple. Howard worked in the Financial District, which was then developing a reputation as "the Wall Street of the West." Tall and clean-shaven, he was a caller at the San Francisco Mining Exchange on Montgomery Street, and his stentorian voice could hush the clamor of bidding. While Howard was fond of imbibing with the boys in the saloons, Lillie, never one to sit alone, often played poker with Billy Ralston and William Sharon. These games provided her with a reliable source of mining tips.

Above, Andrew Hallidie stands on the front of the passenger car on the trip up Clay Street toward Van Ness. Right, a Sutter Street car from the turn of the century dutifully chugs past an advertisement for one of the many shops that opened along the line.

When permanent home construction began after the Gold Rush, South Park and Rincon Hill were posh residential areas because of their proximity to downtown and the flatness of the commute. South Park was so exclusive that locked gates surrounded the area. Now, in the late "Silver Seventies," mansions were being built on previously insurmountable hills with breathtaking views of the entire Bay Area.

Nob Hill, which Hallidie had originally intended to tackle with a California Street line, was near downtown yet it was lofty enough to offer unparalleled views of the Bay and Marin County. The name Nob Hill stems from *nabob*, a Hindi word meaning "rich" or "important"—two terms that perfectly described the people who built their homes there. The views inspired the imagination of the prestigious architects engaged in designing the resplendent, multi-storied homes. Each home seemed to outdo the other with elegant paneling, Europe's finest furniture and crystal, and opulent ballrooms.

Leland Stanford decided that a California Street cable line was needed to serve Nob Hill. Stanford had good reason to pursue a line serving Nob Hill as he was in the process of building a home there. Hibernia Bank's founding president, Richard Tobin, was already ensconced on the corner of Taylor and California streets in a three-story mansion with a fifty-foot observation tower. Tobin shared that corner with David Colton, an attorney. Another lawyer, Lloyd Tevis, had built on Taylor and Washington. Charles Crocker, one of the Big Four, was also building a home on the hill. Stanford, Crocker, and Colton all retained Samuel C. Bugbee as architect.

On one of his extended visits to the City, Robert Louis Stevenson was duly struck by the grandeur of these homes and wrote that "Nob Hill, the

During its trip up Nob Hill, the California Street cars traveled past Old St. Mary's Church (center) on California near Grant.

Hill of Palaces, must certainly be counted the best part of San Francisco." Despite the prominent clientele Stanford's line promised to serve, sponsorship was slow to develop. Hallidie suggested that he and Stanford be co-presidents of the California Street Railroad, but Stanford—determined to make the venture succeed on his own—declined.

On June 14, 1876, a franchise was granted to Stanford, Mark Hopkins, David Porter, Edward Pond, Michael Reese, Louis Sloss, David Colton, Charles Crocker, Isaac Wormser, Darius Mills, and others, giving them the right to operate the California Street Cable Railway Company. Hopkins was a reluctant partner, claiming that the cable cars were "as likely to pay a dividend as the Hotel de Hopkins," the humorous term the modest millionaire used for the ornate home Mrs. Hopkins wanted to build atop Nob Hill as a testament to their wealth and importance. She would eventually get her way.

The California Street line was to lead from Kearny Street through Chinatown, up Nob Hill and straight out California Street to First Avenue. Eventually, Stanford owned eighty percent of the line's stock. He hired Henry Root as his construction engineer, with orders to build the most advanced, best looking cable car yet seen.

Root ordered twenty-five cars and dummies, half from the Kimball Manufacturing Company in Oakland and half from Central Pacific's shops in Sacramento. Root improved upon Hallidie's grip mechanism: Where

Hallidie's grip had clasped the cable with a cumbersome screw clamp, Root introduced the lever grip that is still used on the cars today.

Construction on the line and a car barn at Larkin and California started on July 5, 1877. Plans hit a snag when Cambria Steel in Pennsylvania declined Root's order for rails, claiming the order was too small to justify the new rollers required to press the metal. Collis Huntington came to the rescue and used his influence as a representative of the Central Pacific Railroad, a regular customer of Cambria Steel. Huntington insisted, "They will roll them for me. Let me have the blueprints, the specifications, and the diagram of the cross-section and I will attend to the order when I get to New York." Cambria Steel delivered the rails.

Stanford, ever reluctant to endorse Hallidie openly, purchased his wire from John A. Roebling, a German engineer who first proposed the construction of New York's Brooklyn Bridge in 1857, as well as from some English companies. After expending great energy and assuming most of the financing himself, the stubborn Stanford and six thousand onlookers officially celebrated the opening of his cable railway on April 10, 1878, but not without having to pay Hallidie a sum—reportedly $30,000—for patent rights.

James W. Harris, a recent arrival to California from Nova Scotia, was hired by Henry Root in April 1879 as a carpenter on the California Street Railroad for $2.50 a day. Harris would serve the company for sixty years, the last seventeen as president. Harris recalled his first impressions of the City and its cable cars:

> San Francisco was a young city and everything looked new. Everyone seemed to have something to do—life was free. The town was remembered for its men of wealth and beautiful women . . . My interest in cable cars began when I first saw a little vehicle tugging its way up the Clay Street hill without being pushed or pulled by any visible mechanism. I shall never forget the thrill of seeing the car moving without any engine or horse propelling it.

Harris later saved the company a considerable amount of money and time by purchasing the cables from Hallidie's California Wire Works.

Impressive buildings were changing forever the look of the rough-and-ready hub of the West. This was especially true on Nob Hill. Two of the "Bonanza Kings," Flood and Fair, invested some of their millions by buying substantial homesites; Flood's mansion occupied the other half of David Colton's block. When Colton died, Collis Huntington, at Mrs. Huntington's insistence, assumed this imposing mansion. After Leland Stanford's magnificent $2 million home was completed, guests at his mansion on California Street at Powell included President and Mrs. U. S. Grant, Senator Hearst, Lloyd Tevis, Hall MacAllister, William Sharon, James Phelan, opera's darling Adelina Patti, and Oscar Wilde. On the other half of Stanford's block, at California and Mason, was the $3 million "Hotel

The Clay Street Hill Railroad at its Van Ness Avenue terminus. The Railroad originally ended at Jones Street, but its popularity demanded a longer route.

de Hopkins." One of Mark Hopkins' few requests of his wife, Mary, was that they have a yard with enough room for a garden, as he was a vegetarian. Neither Fair nor Hopkins lived to see their mansions completed.

In 1878, Hopkins sought respite from his ill health in the warm climate of Yuma, Arizona, and he died in transit aboard his own railroad car. After Mark's death, Mary Hopkins married Edward Searles, her interior decorator from New York. When she died in 1891, she left her entire $70 million estate to the much-younger Searles, snubbing her adopted son Timothy, who had objected to her second marriage. Timothy contested the will and received a settlement worth several million. Learning that Mrs. Hopkins had made no charitable endowments, Searles deeded the Nob Hill home to the San Francisco Art Institute.

When James Fair died in 1894, his property at Mason and California passed to his daughters. Virginia, nicknamed "Birdie," had married William K. Vanderbilt Jr. His other daughter, Theresa, called "Tessie," married another New Yorker, Hermann Oelrichs. Oelrichs suggested they build a hotel to be named the Fairmont, and construction on the site began in 1902. Many were skeptical of a hotel so far from downtown. But the building, designed by Reid Brothers in a classic Baroque manner, grew into an impressive, white granite, five hundred-room structure, the second largest building in town.

In 1904, with the Fairmont in mid-construction, Tessie Oelrichs became legally separated from her husband. Despondent, she traded the Fairmont for a pair of office buildings on New Montgomery Street owned by the brothers Herbert and Dr. Hartland Law. The new owners set feverishly to work, planning to open the hotel in 1906.

James Flood died in 1889 in Germany. In his memory in 1904, his heirs erected the Flood Building at Powell and Market. Nearby, on Market and Third, was the City's tallest building, the eighteen-story Call Building, home of the *San Francisco Call*.

To rival the Palace, the Crocker family opened the St. Francis Hotel on Union Square in 1904. The building's style was Italian renaissance, and it featured a wildly popular Chef de Cuisine, Victor Hirtzler. Hirtzler earned his reputation in Europe and at New York's Waldorf Astoria. He was famous for his Celery Victor, and the recipe was highly coveted by cooks.

Many of San Francisco's elite—including the Hallidies, the Stanfords, and the Ralstons—built second homes on the Peninsula, in San Mateo County. The Stanfords owned 8,800 acres in the area of their Palo Alto estate, Mayfield Grange. In 1884 their sixteen-year-old son, Leland Jr., died of typhoid fever, which he had contracted while studying archeology in Turkey. Wishing both to honor their only son and to benefit all of

Left, the Call Building, the City's tallest structure, at Market and Third streets. Below, an original "shopper's shuttle" on Sutter Street in 1881.

Mattie Hallidie, wearing a fussy hat, in 1890.

California's children, they provided $30 million and a sizable portion of their Palo Alto property for the establishment of the Leland Stanford Jr., University. Ground was broken in 1885 and doors were opened in 1891.

Leland Sr., died at his home in Palo Alto, June 21, 1893. Jane Stanford died in February 1905 while vacationing in Hawaii. She deeded her Nob Hill residence to Stanford University, and it was used as the school's City headquarters until the building's devastation in the 1906 earthquake and fire.

The Hallidies purchased property in Portola Valley and they named this country estate Eagle Home Farm. The house was completed in 1886 and used mainly for weekend and summer retreats. Mattie and Andrew planted orchards of German prunes, peaches, and cherries. Their property was bounded by Crystal Springs and ran up to a mountainside. There, Hallidie experimented on using his wire rope for hauling heavy loads up hillsides by building an aerial tramway. The Hallidies also donated land to the town of Portola for a school, and until 1951, their gift comprised the town's entire school property.

In the years following the triumph of "Hallidie's Folly," Andrew Hallidie became one of California's business and civic leaders, and he remained so for the rest of his days. In 1874 at the suggestion of Governor Newton Booth, the thirty-eight-year-old Hallidie traveled across the United States and Europe to investigate industrial exhibits and mechanical and technical schools, hoping that his findings might benefit the Mechanics' Institute. He went to New Orleans, where a cotton celebration was in progress, and visited Philadelphia for its centennial. He then went on to London, Paris, and Germany. From his studies, Hallidie organized an industrial exhibit in San Francisco to benefit the Institute.

Hallidie returned to San Francisco with his brother's sixteen-year-old daughter, Alice Smith. Alice came from London to live with her uncle and Aunt Mattie to experience the land of opportunity at first hand. The Hallidies had no children, but they treated Alice as if she were their own. They loved to entertain and frequently gave tea dances at their Washington Street home to introduce Alice to other young people of San Francisco.

In addition to being president of his California Wire Works, Hallidie was also the president of the Pacific Cable Railway Co., with Charles Crocker as vice president, F. F. Low as treasurer, J. L. Willcutt as secretary, and Joe Britton and Leland Stanford on his board of directors. Hallidie was prominent in society as a member of the Olympic Club, the Pacific Union Club, the California Academy of Sciences, the California Historical Society, the Geographical Society of the Pacific, and the American Society of Inventors. He was also a Children's Hospital trustee, an elected member of the Board of Freeholders (which was responsible for drafting a charter for the City), and an adviser to the James Lick School of Mechanical Arts (founded to provide manual training). Hallidie insisted that women be allowed to enter this school—later called the Lick-Wilmerding School—to gain the marketable skills necessary to find employment other than maid's work.

Hallidie was often an overseas ambassador of the associations with which he was involved. President of the Manufacturers' Association of California, he traveled to Australia and New Zealand to investigate commercial opportunities between those countries and the western United States. In December 1884, Hallidie represented California Governor Henry Haight at the inauguration of Mexican President Porfirio Diaz at the National Palace in Mexico City.

Experiences in his manufactory and his travels abroad prompted Hallidie to predict that Europe's unions would one day come to the United States. He wrote articles and made speeches to that effect, and advocated worker education and that the unions' requisites be heeded.

Hallidie died at age sixty-four on April 24, 1900 at his home in San Francisco. Reverend Horatio Stebbins, his long time friend and fellow University of California regent, delivered his eulogy. Hallidie remained devoted to the university until his death, and the entire U. C. board of regents attended his memorial service, as did more than one hundred employees of his California Wire Works. In his lifetime, Hallidie never fully comprehended the tremendous legacy he left to his fellow San Franciscans.

The University of California's board of regents elected to perpetuate his memory with a building at 130 Sutter Street between Montgomery and Kearny streets, and selected Willis Polk as the architect. When the building was dedicated in 1918, a bronze plaque was hung in the lobby proclaiming:

> ## *Hallidie Building*
> ### *Named in honor of Andrew Smith Hallidie*
> ### *Born in London, England, March 16, 1836*
> ### *Died in San Francisco, April 24, 1900*
> ### *Creator of our cable railway—twice Member of the Board of Freeholders*
> ### *chosen to frame a charter for this city—Regent of the University from the first*
> ### *meeting of the Board June 9, 1868 to the day of his death*
> ### *During his last twenty-six years devoted Chairman of its Finance Committee*
> ### *Builder   Citizen   Regent*
> ### *A man of integrity*

It is unclear why the plaque lists Hallidie's birthplace as London. Hallidie himself named Scotland as his birthplace in the 1872 Great San Francisco Register, enabling him to vote, and on the 1880 census; and his obituary in the *San Francisco Examiner* states "born in Dumfries, Scotland."

When the Hallidie Building underwent remodeling, the plaque disappeared. The last record of its location names Jacob Duskin, a junk dealer, who was approached by a man offering to trade the plaque for money to buy wine. Duskin promptly took the plaque and placed it under his bed, announcing to his wife, "Someday this will be worth something."

Mrs. Hallidie survived her husband by thirty-seven years. After the earthquake and fire of April 18, 1906, destroyed their Washington Street home, Mrs. Hallidie moved to Berkeley, taking an apartment on Channing Way near the university. In 1920, she sold her Portola Valley property, all 368 acres, to Stanley W. Morshead, who changed the name to Mirador Farm.

In June 1929, Mrs. Hallidie moved back across the Bay to the Ladies Protection and Relief Society. Their minutes of June 4, 1929, report:

"Mrs. A. S. Hallidie, widow of a prominent early San Franciscan, is coming to be a member of the family. Respectfully submitted, Edith W. Allyne, Secretary."

And, in their minutes of June 2, 1936:

"Mrs. Hallidie invited her friends [for her ninetieth birthday] and all the household and many of the board members were there—about sixty in all. Mrs. Silas Palmer sent Mrs. H. a case of champagne in which healths were drunk. A congratulatory telegram was received from the president of the University of California."

Mattie Hallidie lived there with the ladies until she died on February 17, 1937.

5

Adolph Sutro and Things To Do on Sunday

Adolph Sutro, an immigrant from Aachen, Prussia, had already made a fortune from the Comstock Lode by the time he moved to San Francisco in 1880. In the early 1860s, Sutro envisioned a tunnel to be carved beneath the numerous mines of the Comstock. Such a tunnel would provide ventilation and drainage to the sweltering, often-flooded underground mines, thus alleviating those and other obstacles to extracting more of the precious ore by enabling miners to dig more than five hundred feet deeper.

Sutro pursued his idea with care and determination. He returned to Europe, where he visited mines, sought advice from the finest engineers and geologists, and attempted to raise financial backing. Europeans were impressed, but they would not invest in a project that lacked home endorsement.

In this photograph from 1882, Adolph Sutro, with his heavy beard, is standing in front of the passenger car. Reportedly, Mark Twain is the man wearing a top hat, seated in the middle of dummy No. 5.

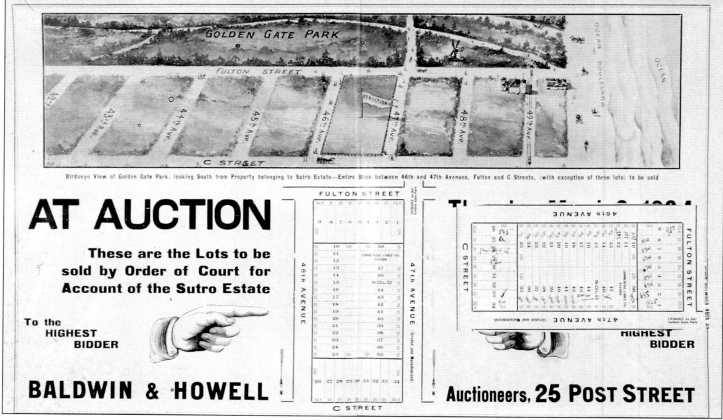

Sutro's "outside lands" were sold off in lots that became the Richmond and Sunset districts of San Francisco.

The long arm of Billy Ralston had reached all the way to Europe and undermined him. Sutro had been in a constant battle with Ralston and William Sharon over the building of the tunnel. They saw his project as a challenge to their claim on the Comstock. They denied Sutro funding from the Bank of California and publicly derided his plan, hoping to scare off any other investors. But a fire in the Yellow Jacket Mine that killed forty-two miners sparked public interest in Sutro's tunnel.

In August 1869, Sutro booked McGuire's Opera House in Virginia City to meet directly with the miners. There, Sutro revealed the machinations of Ralston and Sharon. After heated discussions, the miners voted to invest $50,000 in gold coin in the tunnel. Their pledge instigated an influx of funds from Washington, D. C., and European money houses, and construction began on October 19, 1869.

After nearly nine years, the four-mile tunnel was completed. Even Sutro's detractors would soon admit that the tunnel made the mines safer, more accessible, and more lucrative.

After two years of being "King of the Comstock," Sutro sold his tunnel and moved his family down to San Francisco, where he began investing in real estate. Many of his cronies may have laughed out loud when they first heard of Sutro's proposed tunnel, but in 1880 they were uproarious when they learned he was buying sand dunes.

But Sutro's long-range vision served him well again. The sand dunes Sutro was buying up were known as "outside lands" because they were beyond the City's limits as marked by the original charter. He eventually owned an estimated ten percent of the land in his adopted city, consisting of thousands of acres bordering the three-mile long and half-mile wide plot allocated to Golden Gate Park. As San Francisco's population continued to grow and the construction of new transportation lines provided ready access, Sutro's outside lands attracted residents and businesses. The dunes were gradually sold off in lots, and the area eventually became known as the Richmond and Sunset districts.

Frederick Law Olmsted, who had developed New York's Central Park, had laid out a design for Golden Gate Park, which was denied immediate funding by the Board of Supervisors. Originally, Olmsted favored placing the park in Noe Valley, where it would be sheltered by Twin Peaks from the winds and fog coming off the ocean. Nevertheless, he drew up plans to convert the sandy wastes to a park both lush and scenic.

In 1871, William Hammond Hall was hired as the first park superintendent and he was equally disappointed at the Board of Supervisors' lack of enthusiasm. Hall carried out Olmsted's plan and then stepped down.

Adolph Sutro, pictured at right in the elaborate gardens that he opened to the public, always shared his good fortune with his fellow citizens of San Francisco. He spared no expense in providing opportunities for public recreation. Sutro also established an impressive library, a museum, schools for the Richmond district, and a site for the University of California-San Francisco Medical Center. Below is an advertisement for the Sutro Baths, which housed seven pools located below the Cliff House on the edge of the Pacific Ocean.

With cable cars, horse cars, and pedestrians vying for right of way, the Board of Supervisors decreed in 1882 that cable cars sound bells or gongs to warn others of their approach. This is the Neuchin Hotel Building at Lotta's Fountain (for Lotta Crabtree) at Market, Kearny, and Third streets in 1895.

Succeeding him was Scotsman John McLaren, from Edinburgh, who began massive tree plantings in the park.

The three existing cable lines enjoyed a steady flow of passengers. By 1880, their popularity and expanding residential development prompted two new lines to open: the Geary Street Park and Ocean Railroad and the Presidio and Ferries Railroad.

The Presidio and Ferries Railroad opened on October 23, 1880, ascending Russian Hill via Union Street. The line ran from the foot of Market Street, where the ferry boats landed, giving patrons of the ferry—the only means of transportation between the City and the East Bay and Marin County—easy access to the Presidio.

The Geary Street line traveled from the Ferry Building, down Geary Street to Point Lobos Avenue, a dusty road that ran all the way to the beach. This line turned left on to Fifth Avenue, and ran to the entrance to Golden Gate Park on Fulton Street, then known as D Street.

The streets were now cluttered with cable cars, horse-drawn cars and carriages, and pedestrians. To avoid accidents and near misses, in 1882 the Board of Supervisors mandated that all cable cars carry bells or gongs. Their order further stated that "it shall be unlawful for the driver of any streetcar, grip car, or dummy to approach any street crossing within a distance of twenty-five feet without ringing a bell or sounding a gong . . . until said streetcar, grip car, or dummy shall have passed over said streetcar crossing."

The Geary Street Park and Ocean Railroad in 1882 at what is now Geary and Presidio with Catholic Cemetery in the background.

It took 56 horses to haul the 130,000 pounds of wire for Market Street Railway's Fulton Street line in 1891. Leland Stanford purposefully did not purchase this cable from Hallidie's California Wire Works.

The California line proved lucrative enough to spur Leland Stanford, Charles Crocker, W. V. Huntington, and Nicholas T. Smith to obtain a franchise for another cable line. They converted a horse-car line to form Market Street Cable, which made its debut on August 22, 1883. The line ran from the Ferry Building to Stanyan Street, at the edge of Golden Gate Park, via Hayes Street.

Stanford again enlisted Henry Root, who had designed the California Street cars. Root installed brass bells on the cars, and gripmen immediately began to clang out barely recognizable tunes. This new line produced the best looking cars and was the first to have a combined car, eliminating the need for a dummy.

The many, gradual improvements on Hallidie's basic cable car design often resulted in a challenge to his patent rights. David Smith, Hallidie's original draftsman, first made a claim on an improvement to the gripping device in 1871. Hallidie had paid Smith for the rights to the improvement and then secured them in his own name. Leland Stanford reportedly had to pay Hallidie a fee to open up the California Street line. In 1884, William Eppelsheimer—who improved upon Henry Root's grip by altering the construction of the mechanism to allow the cable to enter the jaws of the grip from the bottom—directly challenged Hallidie's claim as inventor of the cable car. In November of that year, Joe Britton and Henry Davis, still directors of the Clay Street Hill Railroad, attested in a notarized statement that the invention was indeed Hallidie's. One month later, R. H. Campbell, assistant superintendent of the railway, confirmed the statement in a similar document. Eppelsheimer actually scheduled a trial to challenge Hallidie, but failed to show up in court, ceding his claim.

After the Central Pacific Railroad merged with the Southern Pacific Railroad in 1884, the Big Four controlled the waterways of the Bay. Since reaching San Francisco from the North and East bays required boarding a ferry boat, the Big Four's monopoly on transportation was nearly complete. They further increased their share of the transportation market by promoting weekend baseball games to stimulate fares on the Market Street line. Cars were packed with spectators on their way to games in the Presidio and Golden Gate Park.

With their vibrant colors and clanging bells, the cable cars were an important part of San Francisco's ambiance. Colors of the cars helped to indicate their various destinations. Market Street Railroad's McAllister Street line was yellow, the Hayes Street green, the Haight Street red, Valencia Street blue and Castro Street cream. California Street cable cars have never changed from their original maroon and light blue. The cable cars were a source of pride for San Franciscans and the object of the affections of residents and visitors alike. One such visitor was Rudyard Kipling, who in 1889 wrote:

> They take no count of rise or fall, but slide equably on their appointed courses from one end to the other of a six-mile street. They turn corners at almost right angles; cross other lines and for all I know may run up the sides of houses. There is no visible agency for their flight; but once in a while you shall pass a five-storied building humming with machinery that winds up the everlasting wire cable and the initiated will tell you that here is the mechanism. I gave up asking questions. If it pleases Providence to make a car run up and down a slit in the ground for many miles and if for two pence-half penny I can ride in that car, why shall I seek the reason of the miracle?

There was a particularly warm affinity between the Chinese population and the crews of the cable lines that bisected the lantern-festooned streets of Chinatown. Stalwart gripmen and conductors, usually Irish, would befriend newly arrived Chinese and ward off thugs who wanted to rob them. In gratitude, the Chinese pressed gifts of rice cakes, fortune cookies, tea, and carved ivory trinkets into the hands of the helpful cablemen. During the fierce feuds between factions within the Chinese community—known as tong wars—when even dogs and cats kept off the ominously quiet Chinatown streets, the cable cars clattered serenely through. The

Market Street circa 1905, east from Sansome Street, above, and in front of the Ferry Building, above right, was a hubbub of activity.

"dinkies," as the cars were affectionately called, were indifferent to rocks or the whine of stray bullets.

In 1884, Swiss-born banker Antoine Borel formed a syndicate and bought out Stanford's share of the California Street line, which was averaging eight thousand passengers daily. That year was also the beginning of the Telegraph Hill Railroad Co., promoted by Frederick O. Layman, whose venture was backed by Charles Kohler, Jacques Rey, and Adolph Sutro. The Telegraph Hill line was not a true cable line; the system operated by counter-balance, with the weight of the descending car lifting the ascending car.

This new line began service on June 30, 1884. It traveled from Powell Street up Greenwich Street to a turreted observatory that sat on top of the hill and overlooked the Bay. People traveled to the observatory to sightsee, dance, feast on crab, and drink beer from the ten breweries at the bottom of the hill. Hill dwellers bragged that the incline for their new cable car line was as steep as that of California Street. The line was not destined to last long, however. The Telegraph Hill Railroad was discontinued in 1886 after a bad accident and insufficient passenger traffic.

Far from downtown, in his western outside lands, Adolph Sutro built a magnificent estate atop a mountain he named Sutro Heights. His home commanded a spectacular view, overlooking the Cliff House, Seal Rocks, and the Pacific Ocean. He planted his barren land with Bent and Bermuda grasses, readily adaptable to sand, as well as eucalyptus, Australian gum, fir, pine, and cypress trees. Skilled gardeners and foresters planted gorgeous floral gardens in Sutro's yards amid Grecian-style statues. The estate was bounded by a solid carved rock fence. An elevated observatory offered an unobstructed view of the white sandy beaches, of ships making their way in and out of the Golden Gate, and of an impressive horizon in every direction. Twenty acres of extraordinary gardens were open to the public.

Adolph Sutro was a tall man with a heavy beard and long, thick sideburns. He often wore a five-gallon hat as he rode proudly around his property on horseback. Sutro was fond of entertaining for Sunday brunch, and

The main gate to Sutro Heights, right. Below, the estate's solid rock fence and elevated observatory.

Above, San Franciscans looking their best at Golden Gate Park on a Sunday in 1904. Right, the cable cars linked San Francisco's hilltops with the rest of the world, via the Ferry Building. This is an Odd Fellows ceremony being conducted in the early 1880s.

the likes of Oscar Wilde and Andrew Carnegie enjoyed his hospitality, as did President and Mrs. Benjamin Harrison in 1891.

Sutro's property included the Cliff House. Located on a bluff overlooking the ocean and Seal Rocks, a team of Frenchmen first opened the Cliff House in 1863. In addition to alluring views, the establishment offered a variety of entertainment including stilt-walkers and balloon rides. Ownership changed frequently, and the building had burned down twice before Sutro arrived.

On Sundays, San Franciscans rode the cable cars and connecting steam railroads to Golden Gate Park for concerts or the Cliff House for cocktails and scenery. Although the Cliff House was open seven days a week, Sundays were the most popular and offered the most luxurious atmosphere. Oysters, salmon, halibut, and crab were enjoyed amidst much conviviality.

San Francisco denizens dressed in their finest on these outings. Men donned English stovepipe hats, swallow tail coats, and sported walking sticks as they accompanied ladies resplendent in long, flowing dresses of silks and satins with hats to match. The cliffs offered stunning views of sunsets glorious enough to have earned the area the name "Sundown Sea" by Costanoan Indians. At the beach, barking seals amused those who came to wade, relax, swim, or just listen to the ocean's roar. Steamers from all parts of the world passed by. The coastal fog was treacherous, and when a ship

Sutro opened the third incarnation of the Cliff House, shown above, in 1896. It stood until 1907.

Early San Franciscans would make a special trip to the beach to investigate a shipwreck, above. Below, more than two hundred buildings were erected in just under seven months for the California Midwinter Fair, held in 1894 in Golden Gate Park.

had the misfortune to run aground it seemed the whole town rode out to the beach to view the calamity and commiserate.

To improve service to his outside lands, Sutro inaugurated the green cars of the Ferries and Cliff House Railroad in 1888, offering steam service from Central (now Presidio) and California streets—where Stanford's California Street line ended—to Land's End. To further challenge the Big Four's dominance on transportation to the oceanside, Sutro also established the Sutro Railroad, the City's first trolley line, which ran from Sixth Avenue and Fulton Street out to the beach.

The Powell Street Railway, founded by W. J. Adams, also started operation in 1888. The line ran from Powell and Market, up Nob Hill and down to Bay and Taylor streets. The line's power house was erected at Washington and Mason street, and still stands today. Sutro later sold his Ferries and Cliff House Railroad to Adams.

The Omnibus Railroad had converted its horse car operation to cable service in 1886, and Sutro bought these brown cars in 1889. The Omnibus cables ran from the Ferry Building out Howard Street to Twenty-sixth Street. Other Omnibus lines ran on Post and over to the power house on Tenth and Howard, and on Ellis to Oak Street as far as Stanyan Street and Golden Gate Park. Daniel Stein, Gertrude Stein's father, became vice president of Omnibus shortly after the family's arrival in Oakland from the East

Coast. Gertrude's brother, Michael, later became the line's assistant superintendent and vice president of the Market Street Railway. The family's stay in Oakland gave rise to Gertrude's famous statement, "There's no there there."

On February 9, 1891 the California Street Railroad started operation on a cross-town Hyde Street line, from Market and O'Farrell to Beach Street, and built a new car barn at Hyde and California. At this time, Henry Root debuted the "California" car—a double-ended, thirty-four-passenger car that eliminated the need for cumbersome turntables required at cable car terminals. At the end of the line, these cars could simply reverse direction and travel on a short linking rail to the opposite track. The cars had open-air seats in the front and rear with a closed section in the middle—the same design used for the cars today.

By 1891, the City's population of approximately 300,000 was being served by 8 cable car companies with 1,500 employees operating 600 cars over 110 miles of track. These were 110 miles of cutthroat competition: Each line had its own track gauge so that cars from another company would be unable to run on its route. (Track gauges were not standardized until 1981, when the San Francisco Municipal Railway set all gauges at three feet, six inches.) In addition, there were still twenty-five miles of horse-car lines as well as two steam lines, on either side of Golden Gate Park, which carried passengers to the beach. In retrospect, the number of cable car companies had reached its maximum point of sustainability. The cable cars' rapid growth ended, and a period of gradual decline, caused in part by the advent of the electric trolley car, began. Consolidation of the cable lines became the order of the day.

In 1893, Southern Pacific Railroad, parent company of the Big Four's Market Street Cable, acquired the Omnibus and the Ferries and Cliff House companies. Now there were only five cable car companies: Market Street, California Street, Presidio and Ferries, Sutter Street, and Geary Street Park and Ocean.

Stanford and Crocker immediately raised the fare to Sutro's recreational area from five cents to ten cents. Sutro was so infuriated that he fenced his estate and charged twenty-five cents admission to anyone arriving on the Big Four railroads, while all others continued to be admitted free of charge.

International expositions were becoming popular throughout the world. Michael H. De Young, owner of the *San Francisco Chronicle*, traveled to Chicago to attend the *Chicago World*'s 1893 Colombian Exposition. Inspired by the grandeur of the fair and the number of visitors it attracted, De Young proposed that San Francisco host a Midwinter Fair in 1894, a mere seven months away. DeYoung wanted to flaunt California's mild climate and start the fair in January when the rest of the country was buried in snow. Despite the seeming unfeasibility of his proposal, by January 1894 more than two hundred buildings had been erected and the California Midwinter International Exposition opened in Golden Gate Park. Makoto Hagiwara, a former employee of Woodward's Gardens, and his family fashioned a unique Japanese tea garden, with trees imported from Japan. A fine arts building designed by C. C. McDougal was constructed to resemble an

Above, owner of the San Francisco Chronicle, *Michael H. DeYoung. The Firth Wheel, below, was a main attraction of the Fair; one couple held their wedding ceremony in one of its cars.*

Sutro's Cliff House burned September 7, 1907.

Egyptian pyramid, and was the only building allowed to remain standing when the fair was over. Although the original building no longer stands, its location is marked by a pair of cement sphinxes at the original entrance. A great attraction of the fair was the Firth wheel, a Ferris wheel that was one hundred feet in diameter, with sixteen passenger cars capable of holding ten passengers each. After the fair, Adolph Sutro purchased the wheel and moved it to Merrie Way, just above the Sutro baths.

The fair lured 1.5 million people, most of whom arrived by cable car. Market Street Railroad, which now owned the Clay Street Hill Railroad, expanded its service to Fulton and Sixth Avenue to serve fair-goers. In 1973, *San Francisco Chronicle* columnist Margot Patterson Doss recreated the sites of this route to commemorate one hundred years of the cable car:

> In 1894, as the conductor called "Kout for the coive" and the car swung around onto Sixth Avenue, cable car passengers would have seen the passing of Bay View race track as construction of French Hospital began. Uphill beyond it, Lone Mountain would have loomed thirty feet higher than it is today. Odd Fellows cemetery, Laurel Hill cemetery, Masonic cemetery, and Calvary cemetery clustered near its slopes. Much of the route along Sixth would have been through sand dunes, overlooking a Presidio that was almost bare of trees as it was when De Anza first camped there.
>
> Once onto Sacramento, aside from Alta Plaza and Lafayette Square, the highlight of the trip would have been the new five-story red brick Lane Hospital built the year before and considered "huge" in its time. Pacific Heights, originally a development between Van Ness Avenue and Fillmore Street, would have seemed posh, indeed, but not nearly so neighborly as the area around Larkin. Stables, horse-drawn equipage, perhaps a fire engine drawn by three dashing greys, might all have made the ride more exciting, but nothing could have made it more scenic. The return route followed the same pattern except that it stayed on Sacramento to the Ferry Building, unless, of course, a car was going home to the carbarns [at Mason].

When a fire reduced the Cliff House to ashes in 1894, Adolph Sutro immediately made plans to construct a much larger establishment. Seen as a champion of the people, the following year he was persuaded by the People's Party, with whom he shared animosities toward Central Pacific, to run for mayor. The popular Sutro, known for continually sharing his good fortune with his fellow citizens, was elected for the two-year term. He was San Francisco's first Jewish mayor.

As mayor, Sutro was not afraid to take on the Big Four. With the help of William Randolph Hearst and his powerful Washington, D. C., lobbyists, Sutro took Crocker, Huntington and the estates of Leland Stanford and Mrs. Mark Hopkins to court over the Central Pacific Railroad's Funding

Sutro's estate included, above from left to right, the Firth Wheel, Sutro Baths, Sutro Heights, and the Cliff House. Below, the interior of Sutro Baths.

Bill. Collis Huntington had sought an extension of the thirty-year loan, due in 1899, at a greatly reduced rate of interest. With Hearst and Mayor Sutro hot on the government's heels, the railroad magnates' overtures were not allowed, and eventually they returned $59 million to the U. S. Treasury.

Construction of his new Cliff House continued while Sutro was mayor in 1895 and 1896. Sutro also built the Sutro Baths, mammoth indoor pools directly adjacent to the Cliff House. Entrances to the baths were at street level and grand staircases descended all the way down to sea level. Exotic plants and trees provided a tropical atmosphere. Six tanks of water, each a different temperature, were fed by the ocean and the largest pool was three hundred feet long. The complex included five hundred dressing rooms.

Victorian in concept and boldly perched atop the rocky cliffs at Land's End, the new Cliff House opened in 1896. From a distance, it resembled a medieval castle or an oversized wedding cake. In addition to dining and drinking, the Cliff House's attractions included balloon ascensions, stilt walkers, artists at work, parachute jumpers, acrobats, and tight-rope walkers. Inside, an orchestra frequently played the songs "Moonlight at the Cliff House" by S. Seiler and "Sutro Heights Waltzes" by A. W. Kaufman.

Adolph Sutro died in 1898 at the age of sixty-eight. His contributions to San Francisco were immense. Because many of his helpers had children, Sutro had given the Richmond District its first elementary school and provided teachers at his own expense. He deeded thirteen acres to the City for the University of California Medical School on Mt. Parnassus. Today, U. C.-San Francisco stands among the world's finest medical institutions and covers 107 acres between the neighborhoods of Cole Valley and the Inner Sunset.

Golfers now enjoy Lincoln Park, one of the world's most beautiful courses, because Sutro convinced authorities that the site was no place for a cemetery. Sutro established a museum at the Cliff House, including paintings and artifacts depicting Aztec, Mexican, North American, Egyptian, Syrian, Japanese, and Chinese ways of life. The immense Sutro Library was a part of the University of San Francisco until the early 1980s, when it moved to its own location at 480 Winston Drive off Nineteenth Avenue. Historian Richard Dillon has maintained the library for many years.

When Sutro's daughter, Dr. Emma Smith (who attended UCSF on Mt. Parnassus) died in 1939, Sutro Heights was given to the Recreation and Park Department. Unfortunately, the only remains of the exquisite estate is the gazebo. But the Sutro legacy is still great.

6

It Was There Yesterday

On the night of Tuesday, April 17, 1906 the Mr. and Mrs. James Ben Ali Haggin's house on Taylor at Clay was in an uproar of activity and anticipation. Haggin, a noted art collector and patron, had invited the great Enrico Caruso to a post-opera dinner. Caruso was singing the role of Don Jose in the Metropolitan Opera Company's production of Bizet's *Carmen* at San Francisco's Opera House. It was the highlight of the opera season, and San Francisco's finest were out celebrating.

In the festive atmosphere the elite of Nob Hill rode to Haggin's house in their polished opera coaches. Men were dressed in white tie and tails, opera hats, and satin-lined Inverness capes. The ladies were stylishly coifed and extravagantly bejeweled.

The Haggins, noted for entertaining in their sixty-room mansion, planned an elaborate dinner for their guests. Their French chef dispatched men to Fisherman's Wharf to select the freshest catch from the sea. Louis Roederer's finest champagne was served.

Upon entering the Haggins' foyer, Caruso bowed, acknowledging the warm applause of the other guests. After downing several glasses

These cable cars are not embanked in snow, but sand. This area at Lincoln Way and Great Highway was known as "Carville" when, after the earthquake, enterprising San Franciscans turned these cars into living quarters. The ones in the right rear even have second stories.

The Sutter Street power house, at Larkin and Bush, and fleet suffered crippling damage.

of Roederer, Caruso sang one of Don Jose's arias. All around Nob Hill, glittering parties complete with orchestras continued until late in the night.

Early Wednesday morning, at 5:13 a.m., as the last of the celebrants were returning home and others were boarding the cars making their first run of the day, the ground shook and heaved in a mighty earthquake. The first shock—later estimated to have been 8.3 on the Richter scale—lasted about a minute. Three days later, San Francisco was in ruins.

As buildings tumbled, gas connections severed and water mains shattered. Uncontrollable flames quickly erupted. Gusty winds carried embers from one building to the next, igniting rooftops and spreading destruction. The fire department, despite its tireless efforts and the help of hundreds of volunteers, was unable to subdue the roaring conflagration. Brigadier General Frederick Funston, consulting with Mayor Eugene Schmitz, decided to use dynamite to block the fire's path.

Impact of the first tremor paralyzed much of the cable system, and one by one the power houses were destroyed. The Powell Street company's car barn at Washington and Mason streets was reduced to rubble. With the quake's initial shock, seventy feet of the California Street Cable's power house smoke stack fell diagonally across the roof, the main broke, the steam supply ceased, and fire erupted. The jolt immediately twisted the line's cables and halted the twenty cars that were running at the time. The engine

Many left the destruction of the City behind by hopping a ferry to Oakland. Once there, they could watch San Francisco burn at a safe distance.

house was a tangled mess of iron, steel, and debris. Ultimately, fifty of the fifty-one cars on the California Street line burned. Only dummy No. 24, which was housed in a one-car barn at Presidio Avenue, was spared. The strong hum and steady whirring of cables beneath the streets fell silent. In the heart of town, pavement buckled, tracks were torn from the ground, and many of the cable slots were twisted beyond use.

Funston's troops were sent in and, at point of bayonet, ordered all able-bodied men to help clear the wreckage. Mayor Schmitz hastily ordered notices to be posted declaring, "Shoot on sight looters or those committing criminal action."

John Barrymore, who was in town appearing in Richard Harding Davis' *The Dictator*, was put to work hauling debris. (John Drew Barrymore, when he later learned of his nephew's plight, remarked, "It took a convulsion of a nation to get Jack out of bed, and the U. S. Army to get him to work!") Jack London rushed down from his Glen Ellen home in nearby Sonoma County to write an eyewitness account.

Enrico Caruso, who was staying at the Palace, later wrote:

> When I was awakened by the shock, I opened my eyes and said, 'What is it? What is it?' I thought it was my valet Martino coming into the room to wake me. I thought he was shaking me. The next moment, I thought differently. I sat up in the bed which was rocking like a ship at sea. Everything in the room was going round and round. The chandelier was trying to touch the ceiling and the chairs were all chasing each other. Crash! Crash! Crash! I jumped out of bed and ran to the window and looked out. It was a terrible scene. Everywhere walls were falling and clouds of yellow dust were rising. The earth was still quaking. My God! I thought it would never stop.

The great tenor later commented that he would have preferred to be present at the eruption of Vesuvius. The Palace, where he had been staying, gallantly withstood the quake but later succumbed to the consuming fire. City Hall, lavishly constructed over a twenty-year period at a cost of $6 million, crumbled immediately, and fire made ashes of existing official records.

The grandeur that had been Nob Hill was gone. James Flood's Italianate Baroque brownstone, with its brass fence surrounding it, withstood the hideous quake, but fire succeeded in gutting its interior. The same was true of the Fairmont Hotel. The Crocker family home, including a Paul Rubens original, "The Holy Family," went up in flames. Most of the other magnificent buildings were reduced to piles of rubble.

Aftershocks continued to rock the City. Fire burned continuously for three days and began to smolder on day four. Close to twenty-eight thousand buildings had been destroyed, and the amount of debris was so overwhelming that workers simply loaded it onto ships so that it could be dumped in the sea. Sadly, mixed in with the clutter were many of the priceless art objects and furnishings that were once the pride of Nob Hill.

Market Street, above, is recognizable only by the skeletons of its buildings. Below, throughout the City, tracks twisted, buckled, and broke.

The curtain fell on the age when cable cars carried passengers in every direction.

San Francisco was ravaged by flames for three days.

Certain areas miraculously were unscathed by flames. Because of their height, blocks of Russian Hill and Pacific Heights were spared. Residents of Telegraph Hill covered their roofs with burlap and then drenched them with vinegar or red wine, effectively staving off the fire. The waterfront at the foot of this hill was also spared.

The great earthquake and fire of 1906 claimed more than seven hundred and fifty lives. The estimated dollar cost to San Francisco was $440 million. The massive damage and destruction brought an end to many of the cable lines. The golden age of the cable cars was over.

Most of the Market Street cable cars that had been operating west of Van Ness Avenue had not been severely damaged, and many were converted to temporary housing for some of the three hundred thousand who were rendered homeless. Thousands sought refuge in Golden Gate Park, while thousands more went by boat to Oakland.

In the wake of the devastation, reconstruction plans had to be made quickly. Former mayor James D. Phelan had a genuine devotion to beautify the City. During his terms as mayor, Phelan had solicited renowned architect Daniel Burnham to draft plans for permanent improvements to

The amount of debris, above, was so overwhelming that workers loaded the rubble onto ships and dumped it in the sea. Below, the grandeur that had been Nob Hill was destroyed. The Fairmont, in the top right corner, was gutted by fire, although the structure held.

It seemed the cable cars would never run again.

San Francisco's layout. When the quake struck, Phelan stepped in to advise Mayor Schmitz, his political enemy.

Copies of Burnham's report were rescued from the rubble that was once City Hall and distributed to the "Committee of Forty"—the group in charge of rebuilding City Hall. Burnham traveled from Paris to oversee his resurrected plans.

Since San Francisco's early development had been so rapid, the City had grown in a hodgepodge manner. Builders now confirmed optimistic prospects that it would rise into a city of better proportions. Architects retained for construction were cautioned to do everything possible to make their buildings earthquake proof.

Unfortunately, time and money caused Burnham's plan to be abandoned. Business interests prevailed over his proposed parks and boulevards, and he succeeded in leaving only one legacy: Civic Center.

Still shellshocked and uncertain about the future, directors of the California Street line met on April 21 to assess damages. James W. Harris was designated to assemble a committee to determine the company's actions in order to resume operations and report its findings to the Fireman's Fund Insurance Company, which happened to own a substantial amount of stock in the line.

The insurance company, in financial straits after the insurance calamities

A lone cable car on Valencia Street is in for a rude surprise if it holds its course.

caused by the quake, offered a cash settlement of fifty percent of the line's claims. Reconstruction on the line commenced that following July. Modest working equipment replaced the tangled mess by August 1, but it was not until July 1908 that this line was restored to first-class condition. What hardware could be saved from the old cars was used to build a new fleet.

Though little remained of the great showplaces that once graced Nob Hill, one landmark that survived the quake was the gold and maroon gazebo that still stands on the southeast corner of Powell and California streets. This signal house was built in 1887 to prevent the newly-built Powell line cable cars from arriving at the top of the hill at the same time as the California line cars, and still serves the same purpose today. A towerman operates the red and green stop and go signals, controlling the cable car traffic at the Powell-California intersection. The lights can be seen by gripmen on both lines at least a block away.

The Law brothers realized that the interior of their Fairmont hotel was so badly burned that they would have to begin all over again. When Tessie Oelrichs learned of their disenchantment, she offered to trade back properties: her downtown office buildings for the hotel. Even though one of the

Helpless residents could only watch the flames approach.

New Montgomery Street buildings was destroyed, the Law brothers quickly accepted her offer. One year later, April 18, 1907, Oelrichs officially opened the newly refurbished Fairmont, which stands today as a San Francisco landmark and one of the most beautiful hotels anywhere.

Clara Sharon Newlands, William Sharon's daughter, and her husband Francis, built a new Palace Hotel where the original had stood. Smaller than the first Palace by three hundred rooms, the new structure opened December 15, 1909. William C. Ralston Jr., was the first to sign the guest register.

San Franciscans gave themselves a deadline to complete reconstruction when, in 1910, they urged Congress to designate them as hosts of the Panama-Pacific International Exposition to celebrate the opening of the Panama Canal. Astute citizens recognized this as a way to make money and to remind the world that San Francisco had effectively recovered from catastrophe. San Diego had quickly been eliminated, but New Orleans was running a close race. January 31, 1911, San Francisco received the designation from Congress and plans began immediately.

Stock options were offered to finance the venture. Charles C. Moore headed the finance committee and later became president of the exposition. William Bourn, Darius Ogden Mills, and Charles Crocker kicked off the bidding. They soon had more than $4 million in their treasury and were able to lease 635 acres, an area that is now the Marina District, for the temporary exposition. The exposition started February 20, 1915.

The selected site was mostly tidelands, requiring months of grading and filling. The completed exhibition featured Moorish, Spanish, Byzantine, Greco-Roman, Florentine, and Venetian art and architecture. It was a jewel.

The Palace of Fine Arts, with renowned Bernard Maybeck as architect, became the principal art exhibition space. A seawall and pier built at Scott Street and Marina Boulevard became a permanent structure. The wide-ranging exposition included the Tower of Jewels, the New York State Pavilion, the Ohio Building, and Venice of the West. The Palace of Fine Arts, which was restored in 1968, now houses the Exploratorium, a museum of science for children and adults. "The Four Elements—Earth, Air, Fire and Water," a mural by artist Frank Brangwyn that was part of the Court of the Ages, now hangs at the Herbst Theater of the War Memorial at 401 Van Ness Avenue. The Main Library in Civic Center houses paintings from the Court of the Universe entitled "Pioneers Leaving the East" and "Pioneers Leaving the West" by artist Frank Vincent DuMond.

Flags were lowered to half mast by Mayor James Rolph on December 15, 1915 when the leases ended and the fair closed. In time the acreage was sold very profitably in lots. A complete success, the exhibition hosted some two million people, most of whom arrived on the Market Street Railway's Fillmore Street cable cars.

A Battle Is Won

T he years between 1906 and 1940 were a dismal period for the cable car companies, marked by decline and consolidation. As transportation technology advanced, electric trolleys, buses, and automobiles offered commuting alternatives that moved faster than the cable cars' 9.5 miles per hour. Over the years, many cable lines were replaced by the faster trolleys and buses. In 1912, San Francisco initiated a Municipal Railway (Muni), when it purchased the Geary Street line and converted it to electricity. The following year, Mayor James Rolph

Friedel Klussmann and her dedicated committee took every opportunity to refute the Public Utilities Commission's claims that the cable car system was beyond repair. At left, Klussmann personally inspects the workings of the turntable at Powell and Market with some of Muni's finest engineers. After this visit, the PUC was forced to concede that all this turntable needed was a new wooden top.

Geary Street circa 1910. The St. Francis Hotel is on the left and the Palace Hotel is at the far end of the street. By now the cable cars had to share the road with a new competitor, the automobile.

San Franciscans learned early how to ignore "No Parking" signs. This scene, circa 1920, highlights the automobile's effect on the predominance of cable cars.

approached the California Street cable company offering a buyout, but was declined by the directors as their operation was lucrative. However, as franchises to other cable lines expired, the City assumed other lines such as the Presidio and Ferries Railroad.

The year 1936 saw the completion of the San Francisco-Oakland Bay Bridge, and the following year, the Golden Gate Bridge. These wonders of the world all but eliminated the need for the colorful ferry boats and hence for the cable cars that picked up ferry passengers at the foot of Market Street.

The Market Street Railway gradually phased out the Castro Street line, until April 14, 1941, when the line was given over entirely to diesel buses that continually met with difficulty in climbing the hill. That same year, an ugly rumor circulated that Hallidie's original Clay Street Hill Railroad would also give way to buses.

San Francisco newspapers and sentimental citizens expressed indignation at scrapping the world's first cable car line. By this time, San Francisco was, as it was originally, the only North American city with a cable system. The other cities that had once embraced the little cars were lured by the newer

The City's work force circa 1910. Note the ankle-length skirts, starched collars, and something else long-gone: a newsboy. Electric trolley cars were still a novelty, but growing in popularity.

OTHER U. S. CITIES HAD CABLE RAILWAYS, BUT THEY FORSOOK CABLE POWER FOR ELECTRICITY AROUND THE TURN OF THE CENTURY.			
City	**Company**	**Years of Service**	**Mileage**
Baltimore	Baltimore Traction Co.	1891-96	7.1 miles
Brooklyn	Brooklyn Cable Co.	1887	0.5 miles
Chicago	Chicago City Railway	1882-1906	15.11 miles
Cincinnati	Mt. Adams & Eden Park Railway	1885-98	3.8 miles
Denver	Denver Tramway Co.	1888-93	9.3 miles
Los Angeles	Second Street Cable Railway	1885-90	1.12 miles

vehicles. Those who held dear to their faithful hill climbers formed the "Save the Cable Car League," and sent a delegation to appear before the Board of Supervisors. Staunch supporters, led by Anna Blake Mezquida and Robert O'Brien, both writers, along with F. G. Will, Gripman Erwin, and Conductor Riordan fought a valiant battle. But at midnight, February 16, 1942, they rode Car No. 26 along Sacramento, over Larkin to Clay, down the long hill to Mason into a gloomy barn. Erwin took off his gloves and shouted "This is the end of the line!" Supervisor Thomas wrote in his final report: "At one o'clock of February 16, the cables were thrown clear of the machinery and left dead on the floor."

How about a fair trial first?

This series of cartoons by Cloyd Sweigert appeared in the San Francisco Chronicle *and captured the essence of public opinion regarding Mayor Lapham's plans for the cable cars.*

In direct competition to the California Street line, diesel buses began struggling up Sacramento Street. This was not, however, a satisfactory solution because passengers had to get out and walk during peak travel since the bus could not reach the top of the hill. The diesel buses were finally replaced by others that were electrically operated.

Another division of Market Street's operation, the Fillmore Street cable car, served as a cross-town extension from Marina Boulevard up the steep incline of Fillmore Street using a combination of electricity and cable power. Eventually it too was replaced by buses, which skirted Fillmore Street, favoring the less steep Steiner Street instead.

During World War II, widespread use of the cable cars was rekindled. Countless members of the military could be seen boarding Powell Street or California Street cable cars and waiting in line to get into the Mark Hopkins Hotel, the luxury hotel that had been built on the site of the old Hopkins mansion. In 1939, owner George Smith converted the hotel's eleven-room penthouse apartment into the Top of the Mark, a glass-enclosed cocktail lounge with a 360-degree view from nineteen stories atop Nob Hill.

Author James Jones, whose first novel, *From Here To Eternity,* gained him international fame, recalled the role the famous watering hole at the Mark Hopkins had played in wartime: "The great symbol of home was the Golden Gate Bridge and the Top of the Mark," said Jones, who remembered "seeing lines extended down California Street filled with soldiers, sailors, airmen, and Marines waiting for a drink and a panoramic view of 'Frisco' before shipping out to the vast battle zones of the Pacific."

Many squadrons left bottles with their names and squadron numbers at the bar. In the unlikely event that any of their members would return broke, they knew where they could get free "instant plasma." There was an accepted rule that whoever drained the bottle would buy the next one. It was their last drink before leaving America and the first place they headed upon returning from the South Pacific.

The cable cars further endeared themselves to visitors during the summer of 1945, when people from around the world convened in San Francisco to inaugurate the United Nations. On June 26, 1945 the Opera House hosted the first U. N. meeting as President Harry Truman signed the United Nations Charter.

In 1947 the war was well over, but in San Francisco a new battle, albeit one of a much gentler nature, was brewing. The fate of the entire City-owned system, which included all but the California Street line, was perilously close to extinction.

San Francisco's Mayor Roger Lapham was a businessman whose eye was trained to focus on the bottom line of a financial statement. Seeking to streamline the chaotic transportation system, Lapham appointed a committee to investigate the current modes and recommend means of improvement. The Public Utilities Commission was the municipal body charged with care of the cable cars, a job they did not relish. PUC manager James H. Turner chaired Lapham's committee, and as expected, his findings did not bode well for the little hill climbers.

Upon reviewing the committee's report, Lapham announced his plans to the Board of Supervisors and the press. Quoting the mayor, the next day's headlines glared, "Junk the cable cars!"

"They are outmoded, dangerous, and lose too much money," the mayor insisted. "One derailment could bankrupt the Municipal Railway overnight!" The papers accepted the cars' grim fate by simultaneously printing the acknowledgment, "We'll miss them."

But Mayor Lapham sorely underestimated the depth of San Franciscans' attachment to their cable cars. He had awakened a sleeping giant. Popular response to the mayor's proposal was, "Junk the mayor and save the cable cars!" Even Lapham's daughter-in-law, Nancy, refused to speak to him.

In her Telegraph Hill home, Friedel Klussmann read the *San Francisco Chronicle* and learned of the mayor's plans. Later, she would describe her initial reaction to the headlines: "My heart sank. Losing our cable cars would be like tearing out the heart of San Francisco. I knew somebody had to do something." Today, San Francisco owes the existence of the cable cars to the massive citizens' campaign that Klussmann launched.

Supervisors tackle the transit problem

The Sentimentalist

They've been workin' on the railroad

Klussmann was president of the San Francisco Federation of Arts, which was meeting January 15, 1947. At the meeting, she recalled, "I wondered whether I dared suggest action on the subject of the cable cars. Suddenly, I heard myself saying, 'Have you seen the notice about abolishing the Powell and Jackson Street cable cars?' There was a split second of shocked silence, before the room started vibrating with excitement. People jumped to their feet clamoring to be heard. Suddenly, a contagious sentiment was expressed to do battle."

The group called themselves the Citizens' Committee to Save the Cable Cars (CCSCC). Edna Kelsey was named vice chairman. Anna Mezquida, who had worked to save the Clay Street Hill Railroad, agreed to help, as did Viola Garrison, Mrs. Charles Reagh, Sulina Ratto, and many others. The mayor and the press referred to the committee as "The Ladies." Klussmann recalled that the CCSCC was, "as the late Lucius Beebe wrote, 'designated to wield terror and authority once possessed by the Vigilance Committee of 1851.'"

Klussmann made the CCSCC's immediate objective to disprove the facts on which Turner had based his proposal and on which Mayor Lapham had made his decision. The mayor had claimed that "cable car tracks are no longer being manufactured, and the ones in use are desperately in need of major repair and replacement. All management can do is patch them up and hope for the best. The cables are particularly dangerous and inferior, requiring constant observation to prevent possible breaks." The CCSCC called on Leonard Newton, an expert consultant on the Municipal Railway system who had previously run the Market Street cable car line. Newton doubted the veracity of the numbers reported by the mayor's committee.

"Don't let those guys at City Hall fool you, Mrs. Klussmann," Newton said. "Cable cars are the best and most practical transportation on our steep hills. All they need now are new rails and a few other things and they'll run another fifty years. Not only are all the parts procurable in this area, but also the Municipal Railway machine shop is equipped to build an entire new cable car if necessary. And, as for the PUC's figures on losses and costs, their method of bookkeeping makes it next to impossible to get a true picture."

The CCSCC's motto was "Get the facts!" Its members scoured car barns, examined records, and asked countless questions attempting to refute the mayor's committee's complaints.

The opponents' argument that the quality of cables being provided was inferior was refuted by Columbia Steel, which insisted that the cables they were providing were superior to those of the past.

Bethlehem Steel knocked down the assertion that the worn rails were irreplaceable. Its executives agreed that one form of the rails was no longer being manufactured, but that another type existed that would fit perfectly, would cost no more, and would practically wear forever.

Mayor Lapham's efforts were highlighted by his ride down Market Street in an old-time horse car. Presumably, he hoped to ridicule the City's reluctance to progress. The horse cars had come and gone, and the cable cars would have to go, too. But Lapham's performance on Market Street merely reinforced the case against him, and prompted such remarks as, "It would be a good thing to have these charming horse cars back, as well as the cable cars!"

Visiting celebrities were eager to be of help. Actress Irene Dunne was photographed with Klussmann. Katherine Cornell, who was starring in *The Constant Wife*, insisted that she "would not care to return to San Francisco if the cable cars were not here." Former First Lady, Mrs. Eleanor Roosevelt, echoed concern.

Help came from another, unexpected source. Gump's, the famous fine arts store, ran two, one-third page ads in *Time* magazine inviting reactions to the cable car debate. Letters poured in from all points of the globe:

> I have always enjoyed riding on the cable cars regardless of the fact that they may be considered antiquated and a bar to progress by some persons. There is the tendency, not only in this particular case, but in other parts of the United States, to do away with some of the old things which, to those of us who try to enjoy the finer art of living, are among those things that make life more enjoyable.
> from G. W. H., Brooklyn, New York

> Cable cars are as San Francisco as baked beans are Bostonian. Keep 'em for Heaven's sakes!
> from E. P. L., Jamaica Plain, Massachusetts

> Now that I've settled down here in Dixie among the magnolias and Democrats, the only thing I can cling to (no pun) is the memory of the pleasant times in, around, over, and under San Francisco—including delightful trips up the hills via cable cars. I say to Hell with progress!
> from W. G. M., Richmond, Virginia

> I have just read your advertisement about cable cars in *Time* magazine. As a former Naval Lieutenant who frequently passed through San Francisco during the war, I want to protest against the proposal to abolish cable cars. My visits to San Francisco have made me feel that it is the most attractive city in this country; part of its color and picturesqueness are due to the cable cars. I used to get the same fun out of riding them that I did before the war from riding on platforms of Paris buses. (I am an instructor of French at Yale.) There are few cities in the States which have definite character and individuality—for instance, Boston, New Orleans, and San Francisco. If you sacrifice your cable cars, you will be destroying one of the things which give San Francisco its personality. There are already enough standardized cities in America.
> from I. B., New Haven, Connecticut

PUBLIC UTILITIES COMMISSION

S. F. CABLE CARS

Is this operation necessary?

Never Knew She Had So Many Friends

oing Both Ways at Once

OPERATING LOSS ← → OPERATING GAIN

MUNI RR

CLANG! CLANG

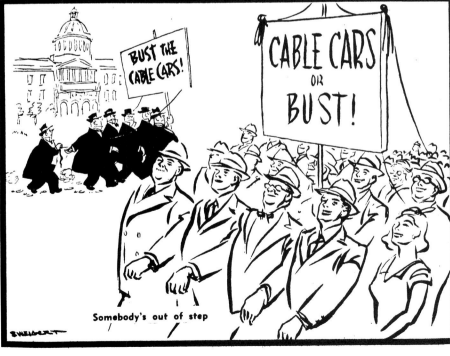

BUST THE CABLE CARS!

CABLE CARS OR BUST!

Somebody's out of step

The cable cars belong to us here in Maine just as do Old Faithful or the Redwoods. Back here with traditional New England aplomb we have lost our best street railway transit systems, only to rudely awaken one fine morning to the grinding of gears and the obnoxious stench of carbon monoxide. If Mayor Lapham ever tries to replace Chinatown with a housing project, or fill in San Francisco Bay, please let us know.

from G. F. M., South Portland, Maine

I doubt if you realize how lucky your city is, still to have such an old thing. Let the would-be abolishers of your cable cars come over to Europe to find out how many good old things have gone, utterly gone, and continue in their existence only on (now historic) picture postcards or in second-hand copies of old guidebooks which have not yet been brought up-to-date.

R. H., Ph.D., Fuerth, Bavaria, Germany

Personally, I'm a little disappointed in Gump's for your neutral stand on the subject. If those of you who have grown up with the cable cars haven't been completely won over by their charming personalities, what hope have we foreigners of successfully pleading their case?

from G. M. Y., Cumberland, Maryland

All letters were sent to Gump's, and Richard Gump replied to every one personally. To the one above, he replied:

> It's only as an institution that Gump's feels it should remain neutral. No doubt the cable cars enjoy bouncing up and down over our hills. They're perennially young and light-hearted. Don't think for one minute that anybody is neutral around here!

The "Letters to the Editors" section of the papers were filled with missives from concerned citizens. One cleverly written letter appeared in a column in the *San Francisco News*. A Hyde Street rider wrote:

> I am in love, and have been for several years. For quite some time, we have met daily and wandered through the streets together, enjoying the City and each other.
>
> Now a third party is trying to part us—which neither of us wants. This party's objection seems to be the difference in our ages, which, from a purely arithmetical view, is considerable. But not to us.
>
> Each day as I leave my financial jungle, my pace and heart quicken as I hurry to meet her. Sometimes, while waiting, I'll buy a flower at one of the sidewalk stands, which reminds me of my love.
>
> Once she arrives, we wander up O'Farrell to Jones and up the hills to Pine and over to Hyde, and up and down the wonderful hills, and past Lombard to the Bay.
>
> All the while with my love, I feel the tensions of the day ebb away, as she points out a new or forgotten view. The air is fresh and cool from the Bay, and my spirit swells within me as, with my love, I view our other love, the City.
>
> Now this other party says my love is too old, says I should look for a younger, brighter, showier girl, one more of my own times. With a slide rule, he tells me how my love is old, if not ancient, and weary. He tells me my love would befit my grandfather's time, that my love makes him think of horse cars, wooden sidewalks, and nickel beer.
>
> But I have seen his slide rule before, and I view it as I would a rigged roulette wheel. It gives a peculiar interpretation of arithmetic. Always the same answer—get a newer, showier girl with lots of dash and class; but no matter what, get rid of the old girl.
>
> The old girl who, to me, is forever young and a part of my other love, the City.
>
> Who makes me aware of the beauties of today, while she delights me with remembrances of the yesterdays she has had?
>
> Who can wisp a cooling fog around me and bound up to sunny heights and spread the majesty of the Bay before me and make the commonplace extraordinary?
>
> No one but my love, the cable car.

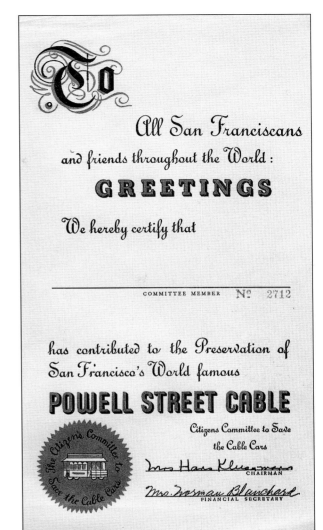

The CCSCC needed fifty-thousand signatures of registered City voters to call for a Charter Amendment to overturn Lapham's plans for the Powell-Jackson Fisherman's Wharf line. Klussmann wrote: "City Hall laughed with pessimism, insisting that 'it couldn't happen.' As our signature gathering effort progressed, it became apparent that the cable car issue was going to be a big one in the fall election. On March 24, 1947, Supervisor Andrew Gallagher introduced an Amendment for inclusion on the November ballot. His proposal to the City Charter required the PUC to operate the existing cable car system."

The Ladies' work assured the inclusion on the ballot of Proposition 10, which read in part: "In the conduct of the Municipal Railway, the PUC shall maintain and operate the present and existing cable car system now operated by the Municipal Railway, in the interest of public safety and convenience, and as a link with San Francisco's historic past."

Superior Court Judge Elmer T. Robinson capitalized on the fervor aroused by cable car advocates and incorporated a pro-cable car stance in his 1947 run for the office of mayor. "Save the Cable Cars" signs decorated hotel lobbies, banks, and store windows throughout town. Volunteers were on every street corner urging support. Essay, simile, and painting contests enlisted school children in the fight.

The Ladies worked tirelessly out of Klussmann's Telegraph Hill home. Determined, yet always good-natured when confronted by opposition, they met regularly and at all hours. Spurred on by their energetic chairman, they soon learned their efforts had not been in vain. When the smoke cleared on election day the cable cars had won by better than a three-to-one margin. It was a stunning victory.

Robinson also won his bid for mayor. "He rode the cars into office," Klussmann wrote. "Yet, even with a 'pro-cable-car' mayor in City Hall, our committee was wary of politicians. We knew that pre-election promises could be conveniently forgotten as soon as the election was over. But, we felt that now, at least, we managed to put the City-owned Powell Street lines safely beyond the grasp of the PUC and city politicians."

The cable car became a symbol carrying the sympathies of people around the world for a city that had been in danger of being robbed of its most beloved institution. Not since the 1906 earthquake and fire had public sentiment in San Francisco been so aroused.

Not long after the election, Roger Lapham invited Friedel Klussmann to lunch. During the course of their conversation, he apologized.

And The Battle Continues

Friedel Klussmann would soon learn that protecting the cable cars was a permanent job.

The decline of passengers caused by the growing number of automobiles challenged the prosperity of the last privately owned cable company—the California Street Railroad. In 1949, voters approved a Charter Amendment enabling San Francisco to purchase the seventy-two-year-old line outright. Included in the offer was an office building at California and Hyde with an estimated worth of $100,000. The City, however, postponed acquiring the line. PUC Manager James H. Turner hoped they would be able to delay the purchase of the California Street line long enough to cause the company to go through bankruptcy and discontinue cable car service entirely.

"While the PUC was fiddling around trying to decide what to do about 'possibly, maybe, perhaps' buying the California line," Klussmann wrote, "I got the CCSCC busy cooking up a Cable Car Festival."

In her invitation to the mayor, Klussmann described a cable car parade and carnival that would "rival

The California Street Cable Railway gripmen sent these badges to Friedel Klussmann with thanks for saving their jobs after Muni purchased the system in 1952.

Celebrating its fiftieth birthday on October 15, 1962, Muni restored its first streetcar to its original cherrywood interior and bright red roof. Here Friedel Klussmann christens the car with a bottle of California champagne while Public Utilities Commission President Stuart Greenberg looks on.

the New Orleans Mardi Gras and the Pasadena Festival of Roses." For a week, the California-Hyde cable cars paraded along their routes decorated with flowers, an innovation designed by Gertrude Barnett. On Friday, June 2, 1950, the cable car carnival took place at the Fairmont Hotel.

More serious and challenging work for the CCSCC followed on the heels of these festivities when the PUC announced plans to abolish the Washington-Jackson line. Despite vigorous attempts by Klussmann and her gallant committee, the cars of this Pacific Heights line ceased running.

The preservation of the California Street line met another obstacle when the company was unable to secure insurance coverage, bringing the cable cars to a standstill on August 1, 1951, and giving the PUC another excuse to stall on its purchase. The CCSCC hurried to assemble a non-profit foundation to buy the dollar-starved California Street system and keep the line running. Money poured into its treasury from previously untapped sources—now many men had joined the cause.

The enthusiasm of the CCSCC sparked other private efforts to buy the California Street company. A group of prominent San Francisco financial and business personalities, headed by Ben Swig, owner of the Fairmont, and

Aboard Car No. 1 on Muni's birthday, Friedel Klussmann and CCSCC Secretary Mildred Bell are served champagne by Miss San Francisco Sally Ann Hamberlin.

San Francisco's cable cars were designated a national historic landmark in 1964, and in 1971, they received their own stamp.

including Jerd Sullivan, Walter Haas, and Cyril Magnin, offered to buy the line. Still, the City hesitated.

Stanton Delaplane, a popular newspaper columnist, stated, "In such thinking I detect the same reasoning that put the ferries in drydock and took the river steamer off the Sacramento, and is trying hard to pull the cable cars off the hills. The reasoning that says, 'Let us be sane, safe, and progressive.' And what I say is, 'Let us be insane, unsafe, and reactionary.'"

The CCSCC stormed City Hall to demand that the City offer $150,000 to buy the California Street line. They then proceeded to lead hundreds of cable car supporters to a rally at the car barn.

"Mayor Robinson crashed the meeting, and was unmercifully heckled by the crowd for [the City's] unpopular position on the cable cars," Klussmann wrote. "The charged atmosphere made it impossible for me to keep order, so I finally grabbed a pool ball and started banging it on the pool table, calling for order. The whole scene was so incredible that I had to make a huge effort to keep myself from laughing uncontrollably."

After a stormy, four-hour debate on October 16, 1951, the Board of Supervisors voted 7-3 for approval of a recommendation from Mayor Robinson that the City purchase the California Street line for $150,000.

The Ladies won another one.

Months later, Klussmann recalled, "I was on a cable car, headed toward home, and looked up at the sound of my name to see a group of smiling men who shyly handed me a lovely watercolor picture of the Hyde Street cable car, with an inscription of appreciation for my efforts. At the bottom were the signatures of 134 employees of the California Street Cable Railroad Company. Tears came into my eyes. It is one of my most cherished memories."

A major threat to the "Save the Cable Cars" campaign came in 1954. Worn out by the feverish enthusiasm of cable car lovers, the Board of Supervisors went behind closed doors and voted to abandon operations on the California Street line from Van Ness to Presidio Avenue, on the Hyde Street line from O'Farrell and Market to Washington Street, and on the Jones Street line from McAllister to O'Farrell.

Within a matter of days, the citizenry was up in arms again and the CCSCC was circulating yet another petition to bring the fate of the cars to a vote. One newspaper stated that "100 percent of the people were for keeping the cable cars as a running and practical system for San Franciscans." In January, however, the Board agreed by a 7-4 margin to slash the cable cars.

Supervisor J. Eugene McAteer informed the Ladies that he would introduce

The cable cars dressed up to celebrate Muni's birthday. This is a rare scene when no one helped the conductor and the grip turn the car around.

Above, an elaborately decorated car graces the Powell and Market turntable. Below, an early bell-ringing contest, held in 1962 in Union Square before an attentive audience.

a resolution to the Board of Supervisors—the "McAteer Charter Amendment"—to let the people decide the fate of the California-Hyde Street cable car system. If the measure passed, cable car service would be locked into the Charter as it was on January 1, 1954.

The CCSCC decided to drop their own petition and join forces with McAteer. They began circulating a petition for the support of the McAteer Charter Amendment. They gathered signatures at the rate of more than seven hundred an hour.

On March 15, McAteer informed the Ladies that he was going to table his Amendment.

"I was shocked and outraged," Klussmann wrote. "'Where is your regard for the desires of the seventy-five thousand people who have already signed up in support of your Amendment?' I screamed. Our worst fears had come true. It was now too late to draft a Charter Amendment Initiative of our own for the June ballot."

McAteer, who had part-ownership in a restaurant on Fisherman's Wharf, on the inner part of the Powell Street line, was rumored to have made a deal with the PUC to give up his resolution since service to the tourist destination would still be guaranteed under the proposed operating mode. The Proposition E that would appear on the ballot, thanks to the signatures gathered by the CCSCC, did not guarantee the maintenance of the current routes as requested by the people. In fact, in its ambiguous language, the proposition actually allowed the PUC to make their desired cuts in cable car service.

Years later, attorney Morris Lowenthal subpoenaed the PUC files and found a letter from McAteer to the PUC offering to make a deal. It was dated March 1, 1954.

"Despite around the clock work to educate the public about the evils inherent in the cleverly-worded Proposition E, voters were deceived and half of the cable car system, including the Washington-Jackson line, a portion of the Hyde Street cable car line, and the outer half of the California Street line were eliminated," Klussmann wrote. "After the election, I was deluged with the regrets of people who thought they were voting to save all the cable cars when they voted for Proposition E."

Using a wheelbarrow, the Ladies carried petitions calling for the restoration of cable service to the level in effect on January 1, 1954 and dramatically dumped them in the Board of Supervisor's chambers. This was just two days before the deadline for submission of the measure for the November 2 election. The Supervisors voted 9-0 to put it on the ballot as Proposition J.

"I wasn't at all surprised that the Supervisors finally saw the light and put the all-or-nothing cable car issue on the ballot," Klussmann wrote. "After all, they forced the cable car enthusiasts to use the painstaking initiative process and seventy-five thousand voters signed those petitions for something they obviously wanted."

Anti-cable car propaganda on alleged cable car financial losses appeared in a variety of media aiming to convince even the most loyal San Franciscan to vote against the cable cars. It seemed the PUC was behind the campaign

This smartly dressed cable car is in front of the St. Francis hotel on Union Square.

to defeat Proposition J. But one month before the election, a taxpayers' suit was filed against David Jones, who had been hired by PUC Manager James Turner. He was charged with "circulating misleading, deceptive, confusing, and untruthful arguments" as well as "misrepresentation of facts to the voting public of San Francisco with regard to the two cable car propositions, last year's June Proposition E and now Proposition J."

One year later, the presiding judge found in favor of the taxpayers' suit, declaring that City funds were used illegally to back Proposition E in June and to oppose Proposition J in November. But the court action came too late to inform San Franciscans that they had been duped again. Proposition J was defeated.

Ridership decreased along with the level of service. In 1961, advertising executive Dane Sorenson persuaded the PUC to allow his firm, Foster & Kleiser, to sell advertising space on the cable cars. Even though the cars weren't carrying passengers to full capacity, advertising revenues would increase Muni's return on the cars. The protests of Klussmann and others, who thought advertising would cheapen the landmark cars, could not mollify

Rice-a-Roni's ad campaign, which began in 1961, projected this image of San Francisco across the nation. This is Hyde Street, with Alcatraz in the background.

the PUC's desire to make the cars more profitable. Sorenson's perseverance not only promoted revenue for the endangered cars but their use in advertising eventually increased dramatically their popularity with tourists. Soon after the PUC's decision, Charles Foll of McCann-Erickson developed a campaign for Golden Grain Macaroni Co. The resulting spots were broadcast nationally, featuring a Hyde Street car climbing a hill with the familiar sound of its bells accompanied by the jingle, "Rice-A-Roni, the San Francisco treat." The City's beloved cars were in living rooms across America, touting their allure to prospective tourists.

Movies and television shows relied upon the cable cars to establish a San Francisco setting. Perhaps the most famous example was "The Streets of San Francisco," a popular television show starring Karl Malden and Michael Douglas, which debuted in 1971. The show featured cable cars in its opening sequence, and the main characters rode the cars during most segments. The show eventually appeared five nights a week in syndication and was seen in thirty-seven countries, firmly implanting images of the cars in prospective visitors' minds.

Although cable service in San Francisco had been cut to a minimum by Proposition E, its future existence was guaranteed in 1964 when the U. S. Department of the Interior declared the cable cars a national landmark. Although the legislation did not dictate how extensive their routes would be, the cars' presence was guaranteed always to grace the hills of San Francisco.

By 1971, Friedel Klussmann thought the battle for the cable cars was over. But another challenge appeared when the Municipal Railway announced plans to reduce service on the California Street line as part of another cost-cutting program. Friedel "came out of retirement." She formed yet another committee to urge the passage of the Charter Amendment contained in Proposition Q, which prohibited any further cutback in the cable car system as it existed on January 1, 1971. Proposition Q passed and the cable cars were now protected by national legislation and San Francisco's City Charter.

Summing up her dedication to the cable car Klussmann wrote: "As I've said many times, every city has its equivalent of its cable cars. Maybe it's an old church or building, maybe a covered bridge, or a distinguished area of yesterday's houses. In any case, you must take pride in saving this bit of identity and opposing the swift plunge toward mediocrity which is overtaking so much of our future."

The Centennial

I n 1972, Mayor Joseph Alioto enlisted Friedel Klussmann to chair and appoint a committee to organize a City-wide party to be held beginning August 1, 1973, the one hundredth anniversary of the triumphant first run of "Hallidie's folly." Challenged to showcase San Francisco and encourage visitors, the Cable Car Centennial Committee strove to produce a celebration worthy of its world-famous honoree.

Fred Stindt ordered these medals to commemorate the cable car's centennial. He originally had them imprinted with August 1, 1973, but changed them to reflect the correct date of August 2.

Klussmann enlisted historian Albert Shumate, M.D., and Robert Gros, a vice president of Pacific Gas & Electricity, to be co-chairmen of this committee. Special events coordinator Charlotte Mailliard announced the first event, a party in the car barn with a fashion show by I. Magnin. John Carrodus, general manager of the Mark Hopkins, provided an elaborate buffet, replete with ice carvings of cable cars. Bill Blass unveiled the new uniform that he designed for the Muni gripmen and conductors, and models included Assemblyman Willie Brown, columnist Herb

Attendees at the centennial kickoff at the car barn included, from left, Cyril Magnin (of Joseph Magnin stores), Charlotte Mailliard, and Mayor Joseph Alioto.

Caen, and restaurateur Enrico Banducci. Mrs. Bing Crosby attended as part of an act presented by the American Conservatory Theater.

Fred Stindt, president of the Railway and Locomotive Historical Society, planned to re-enact Hallidie's original trip. The Historical Society had one of Hallidie's original cars, "Old No. 8," and although cable cars no longer ran on Clay Street, Stindt arranged to put the car on a flatbed truck and drive it there. He also insisted that the commemorative run take place at five a.m. Stindt arranged the trip for August 1, and ordered commemorative medals in bronze and silver depicting the old car and the centennial dates.

Bob Gros arranged for posters depicting the theme car and the centennial information to be displayed on all Muni vehicles and ran a story about the celebration in the PG&E newsletter, sent to more than three million users. Business liaison Chris Stritzinger, general manager of Gump's, provided enlarged historic pictures to be showcased in store windows throughout the City. Historian Gladys Hansen staged a two-month exhibition of old photographs depicting the beginnings of the cable car at San Francisco's Main Library.

The actual date of the centennial was called into question when Rev. John McGloin, a professor of history at the University of San Francisco, discovered during his own research that the newspapers of 1873 named the date of the first run as August 2. Dr. Shumate, apprised of McGloin's discovery, checked in the San Francisco Library and advised the committee that the original date was indeed August 2, and the date was officially changed. Stindt corrected the commemorative medals to show the date as August 2 and announcements were made accordingly.

On July 29, renowned orchestra leader Arthur Fiedler was scheduled to conduct the San Francisco Symphony Orchestra at Stern Grove, a clearing in a eucalyptus forest in the Sunset district at Nineteenth Avenue and Sloat Boulevard.

Fiedler always drew capacity crowds and this day was no exception. In honor of the cable car, Fiedler invited cable car gripman Al Davison, three-

San Franciscans were proud to say they partook in the centennial festivities.

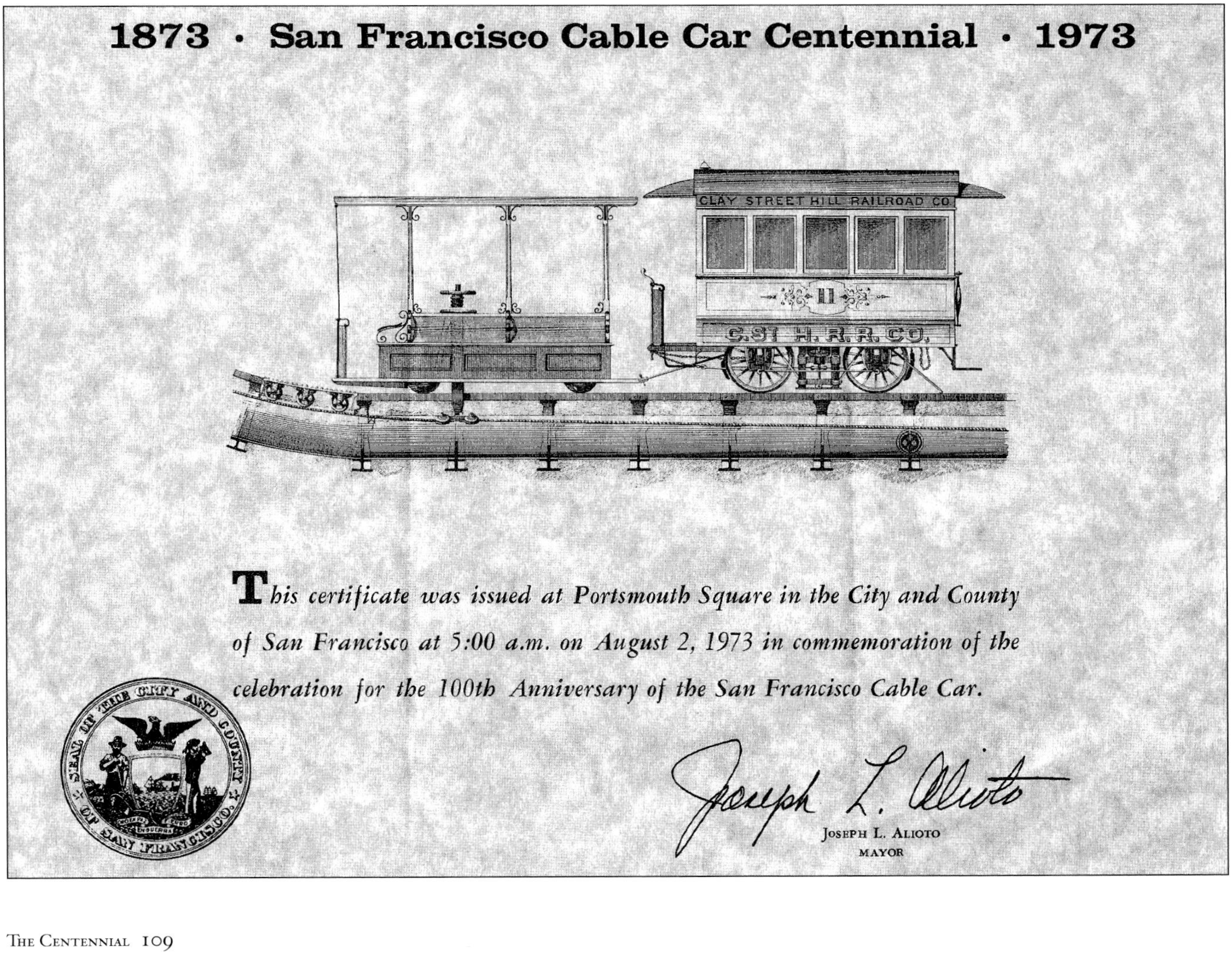

1873 · **San Francisco Cable Car Centennial** · 1973

This certificate was issued at Portsmouth Square in the City and County of San Francisco at 5:00 a.m. on August 2, 1973 in commemoration of the celebration for the 100th Anniversary of the San Francisco Cable Car.

Joseph L. Alioto
JOSEPH L. ALIOTO
MAYOR

Above, this car, at Victorian Park, was decorated by the Hyatt Hotel to honor President Ulysses Grant, who was president in 1873. At right, the celebrations went on all over town, including on cable car routes that no longer existed.

CABLE CAR CENTENNIAL

1873 - - 1973

Honoring those who walked with
Margot Patterson Doss
over the original route of the
Clay Street Cable Car Line

Sunday, August 5, 1973

San Francisco Chronicle

time winner of the Annual Bell Ringing Contest, to play the bells just as he did on the Hyde Street Line. The contest started in 1961 and is held every summer in Union Square. The gripmen compete for varying prizes, and hold the winner in highest regard. Davison was never shy when serenading his passengers, or even when competing in Union Square, but when he learned that twenty-three thousand people would be watching him at Stern Grove, his knees began to shake. But he gathered his resolve and his contribution to "The Fireball Polka" by Strauss earned him a standing ovation from the audience.

Fiedler likely picked that particular number because he was a renowned fire buff. Whenever in San Francisco, Fiedler would stay at the Mark Hopkins Hotel, where they kept a fire-engine red bedspread on hand for the distinguished fire buff who would run outside every time he heard a fire alarm.

Dr. George Rahilly, a Fort Lauderdale-based cable car buff, donated fifty-seven scale models of various cable cars that had been used since 1873. The cars are on display today at the Cable Car Museum.

The mighty men of Muni—the carpenters, blacksmiths, machinists, and pattern makers working in the Muni's own Elkton Shops—quietly and proudly built a new cable car under Foreman Carpenter Archie Kidd. By studying old manuals, they patterned it after a Powell Street car circa 1887. It would be named Car No. 1 and would lead the parade of decorated cars on August 2.

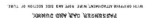

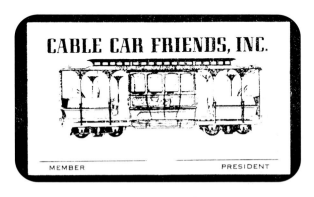

Top, a special label of Hanns Kornell champagne in honor of the cable cars. Above, the Cable Car Friends' creed read "I believe that cable cars are indispensible atmosphere, and typical of the things that make our City different." Left, characters in San Francisco history are represented at the kickoff party by Huntley Soyster (Emperor Norton), Charlotte Mailliard (Lotta Crabtree), and Cynthia Soyster (Lillie Hitchcock Coit).

This car, sponsored by Gump's, honored Friedel Klussmann and her efforts to save the cable cars.

A handful of die-hards assisted in maneuvering Old No. 8 onto a flatbed truck and the museum piece was moved to Taylor and Clay Street, where Fred Stindt was waiting, dressed as Andrew Hallidie. He wore a frock coat and top hat and pasted sideburns and whiskers on his face. Also there were Mayor Joe Alioto and Friedel Klussmann.

At precisely five a.m., as the first rays of sunlight mixed with the fog, they began their descent down Clay Street. Along Clay Street shades began rising, heads appeared in windows, and cheers were heard. A U. S. Navy color guard and motorcycle police provided an escort. As this procession approached its destination at Portsmouth Square, Robert Charles from St. Tropez, a well-known French restaurateur, appeared in a second-floor window wearing a red flannel nightcap. He tossed a faded red, white and blue bouquet as the celebrants yelled their lungs out in efforts to stay warm.

People costumed as Mark Twain, Lillie Hitchcock Coit, and other luminaries of the City's past mingled with stockbrokers taking in the event on their way to work. In tribute to Hallidie, their Scottish compatriot, the Black Raven Pipe Band played. Everyone present received a parchment certificate recognizing their attendance.

At 10:30 a.m., as trumpets blared, Car No. 1 led the parade of brilliantly decorated cars. Gripman Bill McPartland, who had been selected Cable Car Man of the Year, served as grip on Car No. 1. Riders included Klussmann and Mayor Alioto. Hundreds of school children, waving flags and banners, lined Hyde Street.

The Hyde Street line culminates in a turntable at Victorian Square, near Aquatic Park. The U. S. Sixth Army and Capuchino High School marching bands played there, barely audible above the ovations. Police had to clear the turntables of onlookers. On the return trip, all McPartland could see as he reached the crest of Nob Hill at California and Powell was a sea of people.

The next day, Union Square cordially invited the entire public to an old-fashioned ice cream social. Three stores—the City of Paris, Liberty House, and Rhodes—donated six-tiered cakes.

Bob Farrell, president of Farrell's Ice Cream, contributed the ice cream. Not to be outdone by the six-tiered cakes, Farrell set out to build the largest ice cream sundae ever. He earned a spot in *McWhirter's Guinness Book of Records* with an eight-foot-tall, 1,201-pound sundae. On cue, Friedel Klussmann climbed up a ladder and placed a confectioner's cable car on the top. Luckily, it was a typically cold, foggy August morning; otherwise, the sundae would have melted.

On Sunday, August 5, Margot Patterson Doss invited readers of her *Chronicle* column, "San Francisco at Your Feet," to join her as she traced the route of what was once the cable cars' longest line, the Sacramento-Clay Street line. Her column in the *Chronicle* that day read:

> Those who complete the entire itinerary, beginning in Golden Gate Park and ending at the cable car barn in the old Ferries and Cliff House power station at Washington and Mason Streets, will be awarded a certificate of this achievement prepared by the *Chronicle* as a keepsake of the walk.
>
> Members of the Black Raven Pipe Band, playing music to walk by, will accompany us along the route. If you would like to walk it with me, come at ten a.m., to the handsome little Powell Street railway station building that still stands in Golden Gate Park facing Fulton Street near Seventh Avenue.
>
> Coffee cost five cents a cup then, and Hills Brothers, an old San Francisco firm, will make it available to walkers today at that price along the route.
>
> If you live along the way, put a flag in your window or a bouquet of flowers for us cable car walkers, or better yet, join this caravan on its way to commemorate one of the first lines and the longest.

The regular bell-ringing contest that year was sponsored by the Junior Chamber of Commerce and was expanded to be an International Contest. Al Davison won again.

At an official civic luncheon in the Garden Court at the Palace, nearly nine hundred guests watched as Klussmann was honored with a silver tray, courtesy of Gump's, engraved "San Francisco Loves You." Mayor Joe Alioto made the presentation and in doing so reminded one and all that had it not been for Friedel Klussmann, the luncheon and the entire centennial celebration would not have happened.

The Mark Hopkins Hotel won the award for the most beautifully decorated car and Earthquake McGoon's nightclub won for the most unusual decoration. The Hopkins' car was trimmed with tintype blowups of Mark Hopkins' mansion, cut-out silhouettes of the hotel, and nostalgic photos and carried Eddie Harkness orchestra members. Earthquake McGoon's car represented "One Hundred Years of Jazz," decorated with flowers and jazz memorabilia and carried the Turk Murphy Band.

The final event of the centennial was a picnic held August 12 in Golden Gate Park, honoring cable car employees and their families.

Throughout the days of celebration, a feeling of conviviality pervaded the entire City. News of the centennial was broadcast across the country, cementing the cars' reputation as an attraction worthy of a visit to San Francisco.

Square Wheels, Wrinkled Tracks, and the Day We Said Good-bye

"**W**ell, it's about time!" responded Friedel Klussmann when she was notified that the cable car system would have to be shut down for a major overhaul. A Public Utilities Commission study that had been in the works for five years showed that the century-old system had been pieced together for too long. The years had taken their toll on the

To induce contributions to save the cable cars, an honorary gripman certificate was awarded for donations of $10, a cable car music box for $1,000, and a genuine cable car bell for generous gifts of $10,000 or more.

tracks, the cables, and the car barn. The worst problems were under the street where foundations for the tracks were crumbling from years of use. Muni had done a noble job of keeping the system running, especially during the war years when all metal was allocated to making munitions, but now the cable cars needed a well-deserved restoration.

After PUC General Manager Richard Sklar received the report from Maintenance and Muni Management, he told Mayor Dianne Feinstein that the cost of rehabilitation would be close to $60 million. This was in 1981, a time when the nation's economy was heading toward rock bottom.

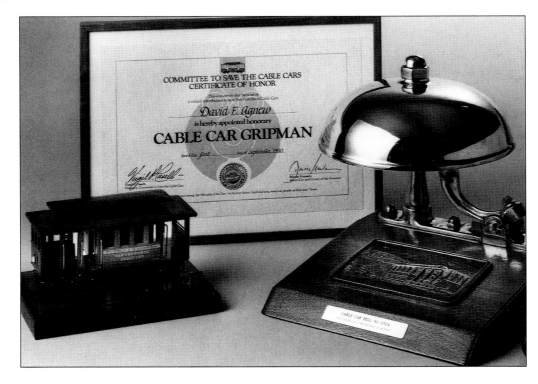

Dianne Feinstein, then-mayor of San Francisco, waves good-bye to the cable cars on their departure in 1982.

Mayor Feinstein and Ken Derr of Chevron, the first company to contribute $1 million.

With consent from the PUC, Feinstein made an appeal to the Federal Mass Transportation Capital Improvement Grant for 80 percent financing under the Urban Mass Transportation Act of 1964. Mayor Feinstein herself journeyed to Washington to assist lobbyist Liz Smith and vowed she would call upon the private sector to demonstrate public support for the other 20 percent, nearly $12 million, needed to qualify for federal funding.

In 1981 funding was approved, but the massive overhaul would take a contracted time of twenty months. The City would be without cable cars for nearly two years! Federal funding required strict adherence to the contract: The cars would be removed September 22, 1982, and all monies had to be forwarded before that date. The cable cars would be back on their tracks June 1, 1984. The firm of O'Brien-Kreitzberg & Associates was retained on behalf of the City as construction managers of the rehabilitation.

Virgil Caselli, chief executive officer of Ghirardelli Square, volunteered to organize a group to raise the necessary funds. Kenneth Derr, for Chevron, was the first to come forward with a $1 million kick-off donation, followed by Joseph Byerwalter of United Airlines on behalf of United and Westin Hotels. A third $1 million was given by Atari, Inc. The new group determined to "Save the Cable Cars" also included Myron DuBain, C.E.O. of Fireman's Fund Insurance Company; Donald Guinn of Pacific Telephone;

Charlotte Mailliard Swig served as the special events chair of the centennial and Mayor Feinstein's Chief of Protocol during the cable car rehabilitation.

Walter A. Haas Jr. of Levi Strauss & Co.; Robert A. Lurie, owner of the San Francisco Giants; Cyril Magnin; and many other distinguished citizens. Their campaign coordinator was Linda-Marie Veth.

Inducements were offered to prospective contributors. A pledge of $1,000 or more warranted a hand-crafted walnut cable car music box that played "I Left My Heart In San Francisco." A contribution of $10,000 or more earned a genuine cable car brass bell with a brass plaque. Those who gave $100,000 or more officially adopted a cable car and had a bronze plaque affixed permanently to their cable car commemorating their gift.

San Francisco being what it is, the cable cars would need a farewell party. On September 21, 1982, the cable cars had all been decorated, and everyone rode free that day. Dixieland jazz and calypso bands accompanied the cars in an elaborate parade. The thousands of riders and onlookers were ecstatic, and many wore elaborate costumes. Alongside the Fairmont, Mayor Feinstein's Chief of Protocol Charlotte Mailliard coordinated a lavish spread of free food, recalling the days of the previous century when every saloon in town offered a free lunch to the public.

At Powell and California Streets, a reviewing stand had been erected, and on it were Mayor Feinstein, Klussmann, Virgil Caselli, Bob Wilhelm, and balladeer Tony Bennett, who rendered a thrilling a capella version of "I Left My Heart In San Francisco" as thirty decorated cars

Tony Bennett, famous for his rendition of "I Left My Heart in San Francisco," recalls "of all my visits to San Francisco, the day we said good-bye to the cable cars was the most magical."

paraded by on California and Powell Streets. PUC General Manager Richard Sklar showed off his gripman skills, which he had spent weeks perfecting. He dressed in the uniform of a Fairmont Hotel doorman. Some people were so excited that they ran up to the stand to hand in last minute checks.

An estimated five hundred thousand enthusiasts turned out all along the eleven miles of existing track to wave good-bye or, better still, to get on board. Richard Sklar held on to his grip to the very end of the day's service, which was about one a.m., and then went home and collapsed from exhaustion. The cable cars were given the finest farewell party this town has ever known.

According to contract, the cable cars were removed September 22, 1982. The cars were moved to Pier 70 for individual restoration and San Franciscans missed them badly, for both practical and sentimental reasons. The shutdown posed problems for pedestrians, traffic flow, the quality of transit service, property access, emergency service access, parking, and utility service, as well as for residents who had to cope. Forced to ride buses, commuters groaned their complaints.

In the late 1940s, Arnold Gridley began buying at auction cable cars that Muni no longer used. Gridley's love affair with the cable car had started when he rode the Hyde Street line as a school boy. Proud possessor of his own car, he ripped out the grip mechanism, installed a motor, carefully lacquered all the wood and put it on wheels.

After he used it to transport Boy Scouts to summer camp in Sonoma County, people were contacting Gridley to find out if he would rent it. Gridley gradually built up a stable of twenty-four cable cars. In 1980, Gridley began a regular shuttle service around the Fisherman's Wharf area and now that the cars were "in the hospital," his motorized cars were seen in many areas. He ran fourteen tours daily from Union Square to the Fisherman's Wharf area so that visitors would not be disappointed totally.

The designer of the restoration project was P. Q. Chin, president of Chin & Hensolt Engineers, Inc. Growing up in Chinatown, he loved the cable cars and rode them every chance he had. Chin previously was responsible for the design of Candlestick Park in 1960 and for the forty-eight-story Transamerica Pyramid in 1974. He regarded his new charge as a great honor. "We had to maintain a delicate balance between restoration and innovation. We used new materials, but saved the tradition," Chin commented.

Fred Kreitzberg, principal with O'Brien-Kreitzberg, the construction management firm handling this project, observed, "There was no resistance to the cable car project. We have had more cooperation in the restoration than in any other peacetime project. Every neighborhood worked with us."

The restoration of the cable lines involved subsurface utility work, street reconstruction, trackway reconstruction, and street resurfacing on sixty-nine blocks. As subsurface excavation began, workers uncovered artifacts of the cars' history. At California and Larkin streets, they unearthed a dank

The refurbished system still looks brand new in June, 1994, the ten-year anniversary of the rehabilitation.

underground chamber built in 1877 that once held the winding machinery that pulled the original California Street cars. At California and Kearny streets, crews found the ruins of a vault that housed the oldest pieces of cable car machinery in existence. It had also been built in 1877 and sealed in 1890. The vault yielded ruins of a huge wrought iron pulley that turned the cable, as well as a major part of a device used to maintain constant tension on the cable. They also discovered that this line, built by Leland Stanford, featured many improvements over Hallidie's original system.

The rehabilitation also uncovered a tunnel that the senior Jim Flood had built from his California Street mansion to the opposite side of the street, where he was rumored to have built a home for his mistress.

Not unexpectedly, tourism dropped appreciably when the cable cars were taken away. Merchants at Fisherman's Wharf reported a 15 percent drop in sales, representing a $24 million loss. Those hurting most prevailed upon Mayor Dianne Feinstein to act. She went on a goodwill tour to New York,

Car No. 1, built in 1973 for the centennial, dresses up for the tenth anniversary of the rehabilitation.

Boston, Philadelphia, Kansas City, Washington, D. C., Seattle, Atlanta, Miami, New Orleans, Dallas, and Houston and brought along a genuine cable car to assure prospective visitors that the cars would be back. She cordially invited all in earshot to come for the cable cars' return. Feinstein also brought along Carl Payne, five-time winner of the bell-ringing competitions. A gripman who owned his own brass bell, he played it with creative touches inspired by his genuine ear for music.

During 1983, to ease the pain of the missing cable cars, the Muni and the San Francisco Chamber of Commerce organized a very successful Historic Trolley Festival. This venture brought vintage cars from around the world to Market Street.

As required, the cable cars were on the tracks on June 1, 1984. But it was a quiet return so that crews and grips could get the kinks out before serious riding began. They had been practicing since April.

Mayor Feinstein scheduled the official date of the cable cars' return for June 21, 1984, so that children would be out of school and could participate in the festivities. When the great day dawned, a picnic and parade began. Mayor Feinstein formally declared that the cable cars were back. She then cut a maroon and blue ribbon which had been wrapped around the first car and climbed aboard, along with Tony Bennett and other dignitaries. Massive balloons were released, forming a colorful cloud above the scene.

Union Square, the center of the picnic, played host to the Stanford Band, the Pickle Family Circus, the Peninsula Banjo Band, and the Modernaires Steel Drum band. The picnic's centerpiece was a full-size replica of a cable car made of Boudin sourdough bread and Gallo salami.

Over at Fisherman's Wharf, gloved waiters from Maxwell's Plum passed out thousands of balloons to children. At Victorian Park, a cable car was sculpted out of five tons of imported snow, and the children were turned loose on it when it was finished.

The festivities around town continued for the rest of the week, and at all hours. San Francisco's magic had returned.

Fred Stindt echoed public sentiment when he said at the time of the restoration, "Without Friedel Klussmann's dogged determination, the cable cars would long since be gone."

Klussmann was known as "the Cable Car Lady," but cable cars were not the only subject about which she was passionate. With gumption, honor, industriousness, and civic pride she worked tirelessly on behalf of her beloved adopted hometown.

She founded San Francisco Beautiful, working to plant trees along the barren streets of downtown, and the San Francisco Federation of Arts, to maintain, retain, and create civic beauty through the arts. Then-Governor Ronald Reagan appointed her to the California Scenic Highway Committee in 1968. She was a patron of the San Francisco Conservatory of Music, a board member of the Civic Light Opera Association, and a director of Defenders of Wildlife. Three first ladies invited her to the White House: Mamie Eisenhower, Lady Bird Johnson, and Pat Nixon.

The light in Friedel Klussmann's eyes and her smile reflect the City's spirit on the sad but happy day when we bid the cars good-bye.

The members of San Francisco Beautiful placed a bronze plaque and a magnolia tree at Victorian Park to honor Friedel Klussmann on Arbor Day, April 24, 1987. And in the Cable Car Museum hangs another plaque dedicated to Klussmann, which reads:

FRIEDEL KLUSSMANN
"THE CABLE CAR LADY"

On the morning of January 28, 1947, San Franciscans read the news that a fleet of buses would replace the cable cars operating on Powell Street.

In this almost casual manner, San Franciscans—who have a feeling and an affection for their cable cars—were informed that the most colorful transportation line in their city was to perish. Indeed, the Powell Street line, starting at a turntable at Market Street, slipping past Union Square, and cresting Nob and Russian Hills on its meandering way to the Bay, might well be the most colorful street railway in the world.

Now it was announced that these cable cars would be scrapped and their tracks torn up. A wave of indignation swept San Francisco. At first this anger remained directionless for want of a leader with energy, sentiment, dedication, and an intelligent sense of history.

It was not long, however, before the embodiment of these qualities came forward in the person of Friedel Klussmann. San Franciscans had found their General. Mrs. Klussmann organized the Citizens' Committee to Save the Cable Cars and the campaign against indifference and short-sightedness was on.

Mrs. Klussmann and her forces maintained that a life and death decision about the cable cars should be made by the people, not by administrative order.

Against odds and disappointments which would have discouraged a less determined person, Mrs. Klussmann's efforts secured a place for the Powell Street line on the ballot. And while the nation, fascinated by this sentimental and nostalgic struggle, looked on, San Francisco went to the polls and by an overwhelming majority said, "Save the cable cars!"

This and future generations are in the debt of "The Cable Car Lady" as Mrs. Klussmann is affectionately known, and to the timely forces which she organized. Her efforts not only preserved a way of transportation that continues to serve and delight, but also saved the City's "trademark."

THE CITIZENS' COMMITTEE TO SAVE THE CABLE CARS, 1961

Klussmann always conducted her affairs with a trademark forthrightness and dramatic flair, such as hauling signed petitions into the Board of Supervisors' office in a wheelbarrow and dumping them onto the floor. When the Recreation and Park Department allowed the trust of Leroy Vane to plan to build a new senior center in Golden Gate Park near the Conservatory, Klussmann gathered citizen signatures—requesting that the center be built outside the park—onto an enormous scroll. On cue, she and her volunteers unrolled the scroll from the entrance of Strybing Arboretum right to the feet of an astonished Joseph Caverly, general manager of the Department. Not only did Klussmann prevent the building from going up in the park, but she found a more suitable location for the center on Thirty-seventh Avenue and Fulton.

When it came to improving the looks of the City, nothing escaped her notice. Seeing that the Department of Public Works was getting by with ugly, worn-out garbage containers, she found better-looking and less expensive cans for the Public Works Department to order.

Though physically diminutive, her efforts were feared by every politician she targeted. Luckily for them, Klussmann was also famous for sending cookies along with her letters. Yet her famous public battles were in marked contrast to the gentleness of her private life. As an example, whenever someone asked Klussmann where she was from, her simple reply was, "Near here."

Klussmann died October 22, 1986. Arnold Gridley and his motorized cars provided shuttle service from the mortuary to Klussmann's home on Telegraph Hill. Muni workers draped the cable cars in black.

Technically Speaking

All cable cars emerge from the car barn at Washington and Mason Streets and are pushed by tractor onto the turntable. There are forty-four cars in the Municipal Railway and as many as twenty-seven are used on any given day. Each car carries a gripman and a conductor. The gripman operates the car, and the conductor collects fares and answers passengers' questions.

The winding machinery for the entire present-day cable system, housed at the car barn at Washington and Mason streets.

As each car moves off the turntable, the grip mechanism is ready beneath the slot, and as the car turns down Washington Street and coasts a few feet, the gripman connects his grip—as though it were an immense pair of pliers—to the 1.25-inch steel cable that is moving eighteen inches beneath the slot at 9.5 miles per hour. The gripman clangs the brass bell to alert pedestrian and auto traffic. The bell hangs on the ceiling of each car and the gripman sounds it by pulling the cord dangling near his left shoulder.

The grip weighs 325 pounds and is operated by a large lever that comes up from the car floor. Connecting the grip entails pulling back on the lever until it is at an approximate 45-degree angle to the

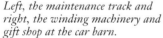
Left, the maintenance track and right, the winding machinery and gift shop at the car barn.

floor, a process requiring considerable strength. The dies that clamp onto the cable within the grip endure constant wear when the grip is engaged, and they have a working life of only four days. There is an adjustment rod on the lever that allows the gripman to compensate for the changing shape and size of the dies.

Normally, the cable travels down in the slot beyond the grip's reach. There are four different processes for "picking up" the cable. The first occurs at dips in the road, located on Washington between Mason and Powell, and on Powell at Jackson and at California. The car rolls down on the track until the cable is passing through the bottom of the grip. At hill bottoms, the cable runs closer to the street than normal, well within reach of the grip. When the street is completely flat, such as at California and Market or at Bay and Taylor, the conductor gets off the car and pulls a lever known as the "cable lifter" or "gypsy," which raises the cable to reach the grip. Finally, if none of these methods are feasible, each car has a hook that reaches through the car floor that the gripman can use to snag and raise the cable. During traffic and passenger stops, the gripman partially disengages the grip so that the cable can pass through the dies but will not have to be picked up again.

Periodically, the gripman has to disengage the grip from the cable entirely. Dropping the cable is required at certain turns, known as "let go" or "drift" turns, and at the crossing of other cable routes. At the top of Nob Hill where the Powell and California lines intersect, the Powell car must release its grip so that it will not interfere with the California lines. A "let go" turn uses a downhill street grade to allow the car to drop the cable and coast along the curve under its own momentum until the straight-away, where it will again pick up the cable. Meanwhile, the cable runs straight out in the original direction of the tracks, then turns at a right angle through a large sheave and continues until it meets the tracks once again. The first drift turn was instituted at the intersection of Union and Columbus by the Presidio and Ferries Railroad in 1880. Before this, cable cars were unable to turn.

The other type of turn is a pull curve. Invented by George Duncan in Dunedin, New Zealand in 1881, this curve allows cars to turn despite an uphill street grade. The pull turn uses a system of horizontal pulleys to allow the cable to maneuver a car through the turn. It was first used in San Francisco by the Sutter Street Railroad in 1882.

In order to prevent cable damage where the rope must be dropped (such as at crossings, "let go" curves, terminals, and so forth), bumper bars are provided that will forcibly pull the cable from the grip should the gripman fail to "drop the rope" in time. Since damage frequently results when this happens, the cable automatically stops. A glass tube of white paint is broken by the engaged grip, splattering paint on the grip of the offending gripman's car and identifying the culprit.

The Cable Car Museum is open daily with no admission charge.

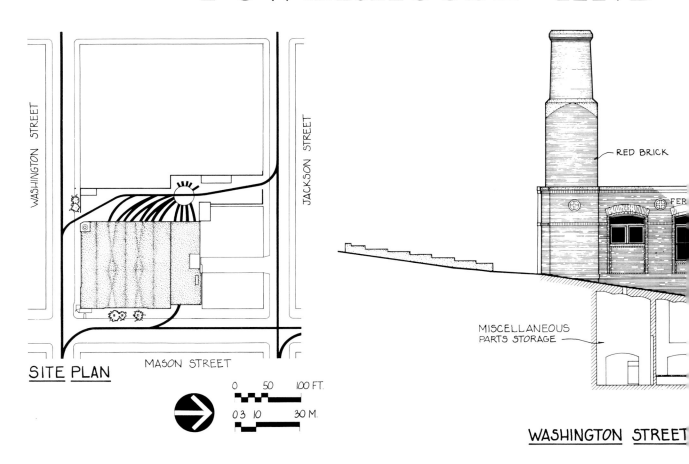

SITE PLAN

MASON STREET

WASHINGTON STREET

JACKSON STREET

0 50 100 FT.

0 3 10 30 M.

RED BRICK

FER

MISCELLANEOUS
PARTS STORAGE

WASHINGTON STREET

SAN FRANCISCO'S THREE SURVIVING CABLE CAR ROUTES ALL OPERATE OUT OF THIS TWO-STORY BRICK BUILDING. ERECTED IN 1907-08, THIS STRUCTURE REPLACED A THREE-STORY BRICK POWERHOUSE AND CAR BARN BUILT IN 1887-89 BY THE FERRIES & CLIFF HOUSE RAILWAY AND DESTROYED BY THE EARTHQUAKE AND FIRE IN APRIL 1906. THE PRESENT EDIFICE, CONSTRUCTED AT A COST OF $75,000, WAS BUILT ON THE FOOTINGS AND FOUNDATIONS OF THE ORIGINAL BUILDING.

THE FIRST FLOOR HOUSES THE WINDING MACHINERY FOR THE THREE CABLES AND THEIR ASSOCIATED DRIVE MOTORS, CONVERTED FROM STEAM TO ELECTRICITY IN 1911. A MACHINE SHOP IS ALSO LOCATED ON THIS FLOOR. THE CABLES ENTER AND EXIT THE BUILDING THROUGH A SHEAVE VAULT LOCAT-

ED UNDER THE SIDEWALK AT THE SOUTHEAST CORNER OF THE BUILDING. TRACKS FOR CAR STORAGE AND REPAIR, THREE CAR REPAIR PITS, AND OFFICES OCCUPY THE SECOND FLOOR. THE POWERHOUSE IS BUILT INTO THE SLOPE OF A HILL, SO THAT THE REAR OF THE SECOND FLOOR OPENS ONTO A YARD WITH SEVERAL OUTBUILDINGS, A TURNTABLE, AND A NUMBER OF TRACKS. THE TURNTABLE IS USED TO SPOT INCOMING CARS ONTO THE REPAIR AND STORAGE TRACKS, AND TO DIRECT OUTBOUND CARS ONTO THE STREET. THE ORIGINAL BUILDING HANDLED CARS BY MEANS OF TRANSFER TABLES ON THE TWO UPPER FLOORS INSTEAD OF WITH A TURNTABLE.

THE BUILDING HAS UNDERGONE FEW MAJOR STRUC-TURAL CHANGES SINCE 1907. IN 1956-7, WHEN THE

E RAILWAY CO.
AR BARN

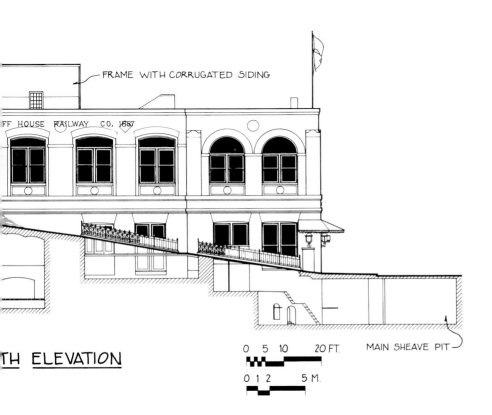

FRAME WITH CORRUGATED SIDING

FF HOUSE RAILWAY CO. 1887

TH ELEVATION

| 0 | 5 | 10 | 20 FT. |

| 0 | 1 | 2 | 5 M. |

MAIN SHEAVE PIT

OPERATION OF THE CALIFORNIA STREET CABLE WAS IN-
CORPORATED INTO THE BUILDING, A CONCRETE SLAB
WAS POURED OVER THE FORMER BOILER PITS ALONG THE SOUTH
WALL OF THE FIRST FLOOR. INCORPORATION OF A MUSEUM
AND VISITOR'S GALLERY IN 1967 REQUIRED CONSTRUCTION OF
A MEZZANINE ALONG THE BUILDING'S SOUTH WALL. THIS
WORK ALSO INCLUDED THE CONVERSION OF THE SOUTHERNMOST
WINDOW ON THE MASON STREET FACADE INTO A DOORWAY
PROVIDING ACCESS TO THE MEZZANINE. OTHER ALTER-
ATIONS MADE AS A RESULT OF THE MUSEUM INCLUDE A
DECORATIVE CANOPY AT THE BUILDING'S SOUTHEAST COR-
NER, THE FLAGPOLES ON THE ROOF, AND VARIOUS
SIGNS AND FITTINGS INTENDED TO CONVEY A SENSE
OF THE BUILDING'S AGE AND FUNCTION.

DELINEATED BY: SCOTT DOLPH, 1981

CABLE CAR RECORDING PROJECT
OFFICE OF ARCHEOLOGY AND HISTORIC PRESERVATION
HERITAGE CONSERVATION AND RECREATION SERVICE
UNITED STATES DEPARTMENT OF THE INTERIOR

SAN FRANCISCO CABLE RAILWAY (UNITED RAILROADS of SAN FRANCISCO): CABLE CAR POWERHOUSE and BARN
1201 MASON STREET
SAN FRANCISCO

SAN FRANCISCO   CALIFORNIA

IF REPRODUCED, PLEASE CREDIT: HISTORIC AMERICAN ENGINEERING RECORD, HERITAGE CONSERVATION & RECREATION SERVICE, NAME OF DELINEATOR, DATE OF THE DRAWING

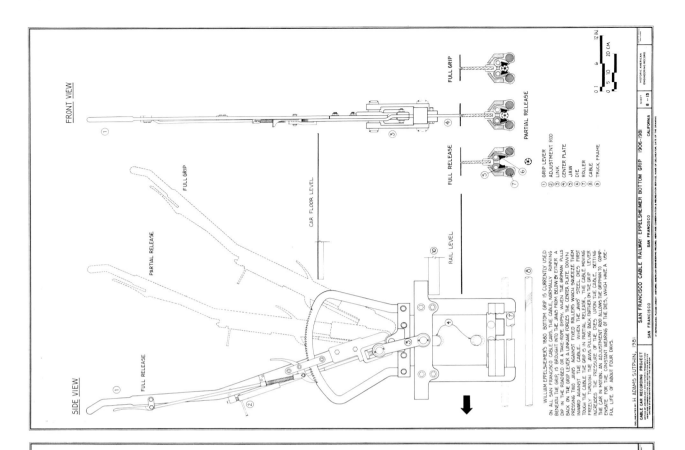
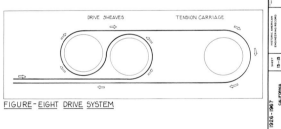
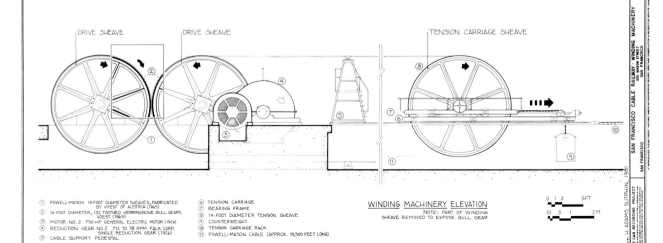

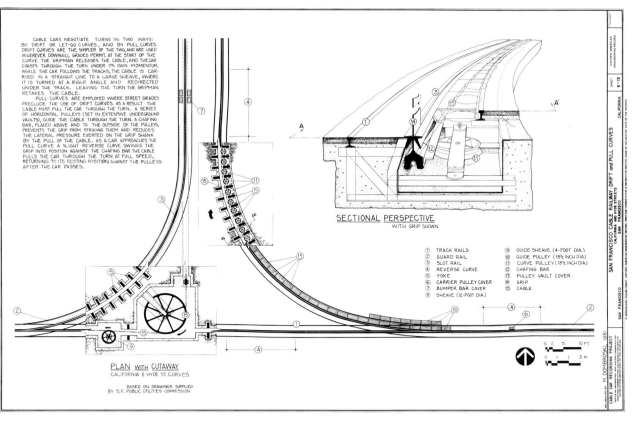

CABLE CARS NEGOTIATE TURNS IN TWO WAYS: BY DRIFT OR LET-GO CURVES, AND BY PULL CURVES. DRIFT CURVES ARE THE SIMPLER OF THE TWO, AND ARE USED WHEREVER DOWNHILL GRADES PERMIT. AT THE START OF THE CURVE, THE GRIPMAN RELEASES THE CABLE, AND THE CAR COASTS THROUGH THE TURN UNDER ITS OWN MOMENTUM. WHILE THE CAR FOLLOWS THE TRACKS, THE CABLE IS CAR-RIED IN A STRAIGHT LINE TO A LARGE SHEAVE, WHERE IT IS TURNED AT A RIGHT ANGLE AND REDIRECTED UNDER THE TRACK. LEAVING THE TURN THE GRIPMAN RETAKES THE CABLE.

PULL CURVES ARE EMPLOYED WHERE STREET GRADES PRECLUDE THE USE OF DRIFT CURVES. AS A RESULT THE CABLE MUST PULL THE CAR THROUGH THE TURN. A SERIES OF HORIZONTAL PULLEYS (SET IN EXTENSIVE UNDERGROUND VAULTS), GUIDE THE CABLE THROUGH THE TURN. A CHAFING BAR, PLACED ABOVE AND TO THE OUTSIDE OF THE PULLEYS, PREVENTS THE GRIP FROM STRIKING THEM AND REDUCES THE LATERAL PRESSURE EXERTED ON THE GRIP SHANK BY THE PULL OF THE CABLE. AS A CAR APPROACHES THE PULL CURVE A SLIGHT REVERSE CURVE SWINGS THE GRIP INTO POSITION AGAINST THE CHAFING BAR. THE CABLE PULLS THE CAR THROUGH THE TURN AT FULL SPEED, RETURNING TO ITS RESTING POSITION AGAINST THE PULLEYS AFTER THE CAR PASSES.

SECTIONAL PERSPECTIVE
WITH GRIP SHOWN

① TRACK RAILS
② GUARD RAIL
③ SLOT RAIL
④ REVERSE CURVE
⑤ YOKE
⑥ CARRIER PULLEY COVER
⑦ BUMPER BAR COVER
⑧ SHEAVE (12-FOOT DIA.)
⑨ GUIDE SHEAVE (4-FOOT DIA.)
⑩ GUIDE PULLEY (18½ INCH DIA.)
⑪ CURVE PULLEY (18½ INCH DIA.)
⑫ CHAFING BAR
⑬ PULLEY VAULT COVER
⑭ GRIP
⑮ CABLE

PLAN WITH CUTAWAY
CALIFORNIA & HYDE ST. CURVES

BASED ON DRAWINGS SUPPLIED
BY S.F. PUBLIC UTILITIES COMMISSION

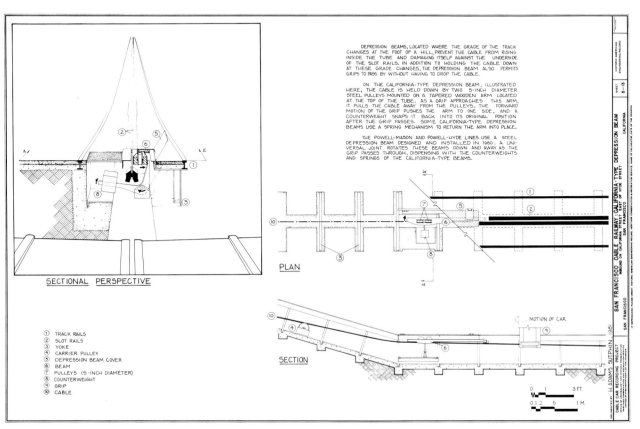

DEPRESSION BEAMS, LOCATED WHERE THE GRADE OF THE TRACK CHANGES AT THE FOOT OF A HILL, PREVENT THE CABLE FROM RISING INSIDE THE TUBE AND DAMAGING ITSELF AGAINST THE UNDERSIDE OF THE SLOT RAILS. IN ADDITION TO HOLDING THE CABLE DOWN AT THESE GRADE CHANGES, THE DEPRESSION BEAM ALSO PERMITS GRIPS TO PASS BY WITHOUT HAVING TO DROP THE CABLE.

ON THE CALIFORNIA-TYPE DEPRESSION BEAM, ILLUSTRATED HERE, THE CABLE IS HELD DOWN BY TWO 5-INCH DIAMETER STEEL PULLEYS MOUNTED ON A TAPERED WOODEN ARM LOCATED AT THE TOP OF THE TUBE. AS A GRIP APPROACHES THIS ARM, IT PULLS THE CABLE AWAY FROM THE PULLEYS. THE FORWARD MOTION OF THE GRIP PUSHES THE ARM TO ONE SIDE, AND A COUNTERWEIGHT SNAPS IT BACK INTO ITS ORIGINAL POSITION AFTER THE GRIP PASSES. SOME CALIFORNIA-TYPE DEPRESSION BEAMS USE A SPRING MECHANISM TO RETURN THE ARM INTO PLACE.

THE POWELL-MASON AND POWELL-HYDE LINES USE A STEEL DEPRESSION BEAM DESIGNED AND INSTALLED IN 1980. A UNI-VERSAL JOINT ROTATES THESE BEAMS DOWN AND AWAY AS THE GRIP PASSES THROUGH, DISPENSING WITH THE COUNTERWEIGHTS AND SPRINGS OF THE CALIFORNIA-TYPE BEAMS.

SECTIONAL PERSPECTIVE

① TRACK RAILS
② SLOT RAILS
③ YOKE
④ CARRIER PULLEY
⑤ DEPRESSION BEAM COVER
⑥ BEAM
⑦ PULLEYS (5-INCH DIAMETER)
⑧ COUNTERWEIGHT
⑨ GRIP
⑩ CABLE

PLAN

SECTION

MOTION OF CAR

There are four separate brakes. One is a track brake, which stops the car by pushing blocks of pine wood down onto the tracks. The friction slows the car and sometimes causes the smell of burning wood. On the single-ended Powell Street cars, there is a wheel brake that the conductor uses as a back-up when the car is descending hills. The gripman also has a pedal brake, which presses steel shoes against the wheels of the car, working like drum brakes on an automobile.

When descending hills on the double-ended California Street cars, the conductor works both track and wheel brakes in conjunction with the grip-man. In the rare event that all else fails, there is also a slot, or emergency, brake, which drives a steel wedge into the slot and stops the car suddenly. A welding torch is sometimes required to release this brake.

On rainy days when the tracks are slick, the gripman pushes a foot-operated lever to drop sand onto the tracks to insure proper action of the brakes.

Along their routes, brightly colored cable car-stop signs are seen on many corners, printed in both English and Chinese. The cars will stop when passengers want to get off and when people are spotted near the signs.

All the cable comes from and returns to the powerhouse at Washington and Mason in continuous loops. The powerhouse contains four 510-horse-power electric motors, one to propel each cable. Once in the powerhouse, each cable is run in a figure-eight around two large sheaves, creating the friction necessary to enable the cable to move. The cable then runs around one more sheave to maintain adequate tension on the cable underneath the streets. This series of sheaves is called the "winding machinery."

Many early riders referred to a trip on the cable cars as "riding the rope." This rope is carefully monitored at all times. When a strand breaks during the day, the line is shut down until a temporary splice is made. In the event of a complete break, or a "stranding," the line is stopped until a permanent splice is made, and in the meantime shuttle buses maintain service on the route.

An ingenious alarm system, consisting of a U-shaped fork that hugs the moving cable and is connected to a locator board at the car barn, alerts the maintenance crew to the possibility of a wire that has broken loose from the thick-woven cable. In addition to the four alarms in the basement tunnels of the car barn—one for each cable—there are more than sixty strand alarms located throughout the system, usually one every block or two. Any foreign object or projection from the cable passing through the strand alarm triggers a computer operated control system that automatically shuts down the line. All cable machinery halts and the broken strand is located by the maintenance crew by looking into the cable slot or raising the pulley covers built into the street every twenty or thirty feet. When the rope stops, the gripmen drop the rope and free the cable. If the cable is undamaged, the repair crew calls the car barn to start the cable. If the cable needs splic-ing, the damaged section is reeled into the barn, and shuttle buses main-tain service.

Pine tar is used as a lubricant for the cables. During the system's rehabilitation, Chevron Research and San Francisco State University produced a special lubricant to replace the traditional pine tar, hoping to avoid the odor that the tar produced from friction. But pine tar is the only substance that can successfully provide a chemical buffer between the cable and the dies of the grip and thereby prevent the two from fusing because of friction. The pine tar also provides a sticky surface so that the grip can better hold on to the cable.

Depression beams are located at the bottom of hills where the track grades change. The beams hold the cable in its channel and allow the grip to pass without dropping the cable. Also in use, since 1991, are offset beams, which stay fixed in their location and deflect the cable and the grip to the side.

There are almost eleven miles of track in the present cable system. The three routes serve Union Square, the Financial District, Chinatown, Fisherman's Wharf, and Aquatic Park. They carry an estimated 13.5 million passengers annually. Visitors may purchase a "Passport," which is good on the entire Muni Railway System, including the cable cars. The cost is six dollars for one day, ten dollars for three days, and fifteen dollars for seven consecutive days. The Passport may be purchased at the City Hall information booth, the Powell-Market police kiosk, and the Muni at Presidio and Geary streets. More than two dozen visitors' attractions offer discounted admission when these passes are shown.

When in need of repair, all the work is done by the Muni maintenance crew. When a new car has to be built, this too is done by them, although in some cases parts will be contracted from other cities.

Many visitors refer to the cable cars as trolleys, but this is erroneous. Technically, a trolley is the little wheel at the top end of the pole on a vehi-

CABLE CAR SPECIFICATIONS

SINGLE-END CARS		DOUBLE-END CARS
12,180 pounds	Weight	11,500 pounds
30	Seating Capacity	34
27'	Length over Bumpers	30'5"
10'3"	Height	10'3"
3'6"	Track Gauge	3'6"

CABLE FACTS

LINE	LENGTH	AVERAGE LIFE
California	21,500"	300 days
Hyde	15,700"	125 days
Mason	10,050"	185 days
Powell	9,050"	110 days

cle's roof. The wheel rolls along an overhead wire, collecting electricity to propel the vehicle. Trolley wheels were replaced by carbon and brass slides, or pantographs, long ago, but the name has endured as a generic term for an urban rail vehicle. In San Francisco and most North American cities, electric street rail vehicles are more often called streetcars than trolleys.

The massive cable machinery and examples of antiquated cable cars are on display at the car barn and museum at Washington and Mason streets. The building was originally built in 1889 as the power house for the Ferries and Cliff House Railway, but it was destroyed in the quake and fire of 1906. The present structure was erected on the remains in 1908. In 1967, the museum was inaugurated, with four antique cable cars and many other artifacts that had been collected throughout the years. When the Southern Pacific Railroad took down its building at Third and Townsend, the museum acquired its ornate gift shop, with the likeness of a cable car made from one thousand amber glass squares in its roof.

The cable car barn and museum underwent major changes during the system's rehabilitation between 1982 and 1984. Visitors may now observe the actual cables in motion, first from downstairs in the sheave room and then from upstairs looking down on them. Descriptions are posted explaining this entire operation. An entire grip mechanism and car No. 8, one of Hallidie's original fleet from the Clay Street Hill Railroad Company, can also be viewed. As of August 1993, this museum has been operated by the Friends of the Cable Car Museum.

The museum is open daily from ten to five, and there is no admission charge.

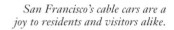

Riding the Rope:
A Scenic Trip

For visitors and residents alike, the cable cars remain one of the best ways to experience San Francisco and see its many attractions.

The Powell Street line starts at a turntable at Powell and Market streets. Hallidie Plaza, a visitor information center, was built there during the restoration of the cable cars as a monument to their inventor, Andrew Hallidie. The San Francisco Convention and Visitors Bureau, which runs the center, boasts that they can communicate in at least ten languages, including Japanese, Chinese, Thai, and Hungarian. On busy days, they answer questions and give directions to as many as four thousand people, and annually more than seven hundred thousand.

Throngs of visitors wait patiently for a chance to help turn the cars around on the turntable. Next to the turntable stands the esteemed Flood Building, built in 1904 as a memorial to the senior Jim Flood. The building has always been home to notable tenants, including the Pinkerton Detective Agency. One of this agency's more prominent detectives later became a renowned mystery writer—Dashiell Hammett. Hammett penned such genre classics as *The Thin*

San Francisco's cable cars are a joy to residents and visitors alike.

The Powell-Hyde street ride is the most scenic. Top, Lombard, the famous "crooked street," winds off down the hill. Bottom, the San Francisco Bay and Alcatraz offer a fascinating backdrop.

Man and *The Maltese Falcon*, both of which enjoyed enormous popularity when translated to the silver screen. Hammett was fond of dining at John's Grill, half a block away from the Flood Building, at 63 Ellis Street, and they still have a room named for him. Tours are available of sites made famous in his stories.

The Powell Street cars run through Union Square, which is bordered by Powell, Post, Geary, and Stockton streets. The Square contains the St. Francis Hotel, the Hyatt-Union Square Hotel, office buildings, and shops such as Macy's, Neiman Marcus, Saks Fifth Avenue, Gump's, Tiffany & Co., and a host of others. In its center is a statue named "Winged Victory." This creation of sculptor Robert I. Aiken was commissioned to commemorate Admiral George Dewey's victory at Manila, and was dedicated May 4, 1903 by President Theodore Roosevelt.

The cars then continue up Nob Hill, where the view to the east features Telegraph Hill, the Bay, and the hills of Berkeley and Oakland. Telegraph Hill was so named because it served as a lookout post for incoming merchant ships. When one was sighted, a semaphore signal was sent downtown. Later, public-spirited citizens purchased this property, which they named Pioneer Park and gave to the City.

Coit Tower, a two-hundred-foot edifice atop Telegraph Hill, was dedicated in 1933 and named for Lillie Hitchcock Coit, its benefactress. When Coit died in 1929, she bequeathed a sum "with which to add to the beauty of the City I have always loved." She suggested the location, but had nothing to do with its design. Executors of her will retained architect Arthur Brown Jr. to design this tower.

The cable cars have always had a special relationship with Chinatown.

The entrance level offers a selection of murals from the Depression Era. A quick elevator ride to the top provides a 360-degree Bay view, making it a great place to take visitors. Though many erroneously believe Coit left it as a monument to her husband or to the volunteer firemen, Coit Tower was meant only to glorify San Francisco. Coit did dedicate a statue by Haig Patigian to the volunteer firemen; it is in Washington Square, at the bottom of Telegraph Hill in North Beach.

The trip aboard the Powell-Hyde cable car is the most fascinating. Once you have hung on rounding the curves, you can settle down and enjoy the scenic points along Hyde Street. When you come to Union Street, you may want to get off and go to Swensen's, where since 1948 they have been serving the most delicious ice cream and sherbet. Along the way are several tempting Italian restaurants.

Left, Coit Tower and a statue of Christopher Columbus. Top, the Westin St. Francis.

At Hyde and Greenwich, off to your left and surrounded by trees, are the Alice Marble tennis courts, named for the world-famous champion who started playing on the City's courts. On the next block to your right is the famous "crooked street," which makes hairpin turns down Lombard. At Chestnut Street your descent begins, and the next block on your right is Francisco Street, site of some truly beautiful Russian Hill homes.

On your way down this steep grade, you will see before you an enchanting view of the sparkling Bay and its two great bridges. When you reach the end of the line you will be at Beach Street, and on one corner is the Buena Vista Cafe, "United States Headquarters for Irish Coffee," which they have been serving since 1952. At that time, many newspaper people frequented the cafe and among the regulars was the *Chronicle's* popular columnist Stan Delaplane. Owner Jack Koeppler listened as Delaplane extolled the virtues of the coffee he sipped at Shannon Airport in Ireland. Jack dared him to experiment and try to duplicate it. The two of them combined their tastes and talents to concoct their own version of Irish coffee. Word quickly spread about their elixir. Today, the cafe serves two thousand glasses of Irish coffee a day.

Across the street is another cable car turntable, Victorian Park, and Aquatic Park, as well as the Hyde Street Pier with its antique ships. Among them is the *Eppleton Hall*, a paddlewheel tug on which then-executive editor of the *San Francisco Chronicle*, Scott Newhall, sailed from England in 1970.

A short walk will take you to Ghirardelli Square, the Cannery, the Maritime Museum, and Pier 39. Alcatraz Island sits ahead, out in the Bay.

Ghirardelli Square began in 1864 as the Woolen Mill, a producer of Civil War uniforms. In 1893, the sons of Domingo Ghirardelli bought it and converted it to a chocolate factory. In 1916, architect William Mooser added a clock tower.

In the 1960s, the brothers elected to move the chocolate factory to the East Bay and sold the complex to Golden Grain Macaroni, makers of Rice-A-Roni. William Matson Roth and his mother, Lurline Matson Roth, were concerned about historical sites being needlessly destroyed, and so they purchased Ghirardelli Square in 1963 for $2.5 million. He vowed to return the delicious aroma of chocolate that had long floated through the neighborhood. He also added restaurants and shops that offer a fascinating waterfront view.

Also facing the waterfront is the Cannery. Leonard Martin perceived that Del Monte's long vacant produce cannery could be converted into another complex of shops, galleries, restaurants, and cafés. Free outdoor entertainment and shrimp or crab cocktails are part of the year-round friendly atmosphere.

An abandoned aging cargo pier was transformed by Warren Simmons and opened in 1978 as Pier 39. With more than one hundred restaurants, most known for seafood, and shops of many descriptions, it covers forty-five acres and is also home port of the Blue & Gold Fleet of tour boats.

Between Pier 39 and Pier 43—home to another antique ship, the *Balclutha*—is Pier 41, home of the Red & White Fleet, which will take you to Alcatraz.

Alcatrace is Spanish for pelican, a bird that flocked to the small rocky island rising 135 feet above the Bay. In approximately 1775, Spanish mariner Juan Manuel de Ayala named the island *Isla de los Alcatraces*. In 1885, the U. S. Army used it for various reasons, including as a disciplinary barracks. The prison buildings were built between 1909 and 1912.

The Federal Prisons Bureau claimed it in 1933, to be an escape-proof prison for serious lawbreakers. During its time as a federal prison, it housed such notable criminals as George "Machine Gun" Kelly, Al Capone, and the "Birdman of Alcatraz," Robert Stroud. It was named Alcatraz, but it was known in the underworld as "the Rock." Eventually the cost of running the prison proved to be too great, and in March 1963 it was closed down. More than three hundred Native Americans moved out to the island to live among the decaying buildings. Their numbers dwindled until 1973, when Alcatraz became part of the Golden Gate Recreation Area's National Park Service and was opened to the public. The Red & White Fleet contracted to transport visitors out of Pier 41, and immediately they were taking one

The California Street cable car climbs Nob Hill as the San Francisco-Oakland Bay Bridge looms in the background.

thousand a day. In the 1990s, it is still a crumbling ruin but continues to be one of the Bay Area's most popular visitor attractions. Red & White Fleet advises that reservations be made in advance. They now take five thousand people daily in their fleet of thirteen boats.

Board a California Street cable car at Van Ness and California and you will proceed to Polk Street, known more familiarly as "Polk Gulch," where cattle once grazed. It is now populated with shops and restaurants. The ride continues up to Taylor Street and Nob Hill. On your left is the prestigious Grace Cathedral, made possible by a land donation to the Episcopal Diocese from Charles Crocker's son after the Crocker homes were razed in the earthquake and fire of 1906. On your right is the Huntington Hotel, with Huntington Park across the street. Next to this is the brownstone that once belonged to James Flood. It is now a private club for men, the Pacific Union Club. On your left is the Fairmont Hotel, and on your right is the Mark Hopkins Hotel, with its world famous Top of the Mark lounge. Adjacent is the Stanford Court Hotel, on the site of Leland Stanford's mansion.

Descending, you will cross Powell Street, where the Powell gripmen must release their grips and coast across so that they will not snag the California cables.

At Stockton, the Ritz Carlton Hotel is on your right. You will then come to Grant Avenue, which leads into Chinatown. And on your right at Kearny is the headquarters for the Bank of America, founded by A. P. Giannini, and once the world's largest bank. Atop, on the fifty-second floor, is the Carnelian Room restaurant, with a breathtaking 360-degree view. It is open only to bankers at lunch, but the public is welcome after three p.m. At the terminus of this line is the Hyatt Regency Hotel, which proudly displays a plaque commemorating the cable cars' one-hundredth anniversary. When you get off the car, you will be on Market Street, always a hub of activity.

With all of these attractions, and many more, small wonder that San Francisco is indeed "Everybody's Favorite City." The alluring charm, beauty, and history of San Francisco currently attract more than 15 million visitors annually, accounting for $4 billion in revenue and an estimated 60,000 jobs. And nothing captures the City's spirit as fully as cables whirring, bells clanging, and cable cars carrying delighted passengers up and down San Francisco's majestic hills.

Index

Reference Notes

The following people and organizations contributed greatly to the researching of this book.

Asian Art Museum
Bancroft Library, U. C.-Berkeley
Bechtel Corporation, Rick Laubscher,
    Manager of Corporate Communications
Blake, Moffitt & Towne
British Consulate
Cable Car Museum, Christopher F. Melching, Curator;
    Dr. Rob Waters, Historian; Emiliano Echeverria, Archivist
California Historical Society, Hallidie Collection
California State Library
Chin & Hensolt Engineers, Inc., P. Q. Chin, President
Fairmont Hotel, Shirley Ann Kantoff, Asst. to Richard L. Swig;
    Cynthia Bowman, Director of Public Relations
Feinstein, Senator Dianne
Fine Arts Museum of San Francisco,
    Linda Jablon, Director of Public Relations
Gump, Richard
McMicken, William E.
Mark Hopkins Hotel, Hart Smith;
    Gabriela Knubis, Director of Public Relations
Market Street Railway Company
Mechanics' Institute
Mills College, Mary Manning Cook, Reference Librarian

Museum of the City of San Francisco, Gladys Hansen, Curator;
    Bob Durden, Photo Archivist
O'Brien-Kreitzberg & Associates, Jane Neilson,
    Director of Public Relations
Ortega, Elizabeth
Pacific Union Club
Public Utilities Commission, Marshall Moxom, Photogrpaher
Railway and Locomotive Historical Society, Fred A. Stindt
Regnery, Dorothy
San Francisco Maritime Museum, Irene Stachura
Sklar, Richard
St. Francis Hotel, Michelle Saevke, Director of Public Relations
San Francisco Convention and Visitors Bureau
San Francisco Municipal Railway
San Mateo County Historical Museum, Marion Holmes, Librarian
Society of California Pioneers, Stanleigh Bry
Stanford Court Hotel, James Nassikas
Sutro Library, Richard Dillon; Clyde Janes, Supervising Librarian
University of California, San Francisco News and
    Public Information Services
Wells Fargo History Room
Wiley, Tova
Zooley, Delphine

Bibliography

Abeloe, William N., et al. *Historic Spots in California*, Stanford University Press, 1970.

Altrocchi, Julia Cooley. *The Spectacular San Franciscans*, E. P. Dutton and Co., New York, 1949, also personal interview.

Asbury, Herbert. *The Barbary Coast*, Garden City Publishing Co., Garden City, N.Y., 1933.

Atherton, Gertrude. *My San Francisco: A Wayward Biography*, Bobbs-Merrill, 1946.

Beebe, Lucius and Clegg, Charles. *Cable Car Carnival*, Graeme Hardy, 1951.

Berlin, Ellin. *Silver Platter*, Doubleday & Co., New York, 1957.

Boggs, Mae Helene Bacon. *My Playhouse Was A Concord Coach*, also personal interview.

Bronson, William Knox. *The Earth Shook The Sky Burned*, Doubleday & Co., Garden City, N.Y., 1959.

Coit, Lillie Hitchcock. Unpublished diaries.

De Ford, Miriam Allen. *They Were San Franciscans*, Caxton Printers Ltd., 1947.

Doss, Margot Patterson. *San Francisco At Your Feet*, Presidio Press, 1940.

Field, Isobel. *This Life I've Loved*, Longman Green & Co., New York and Toronto, 1937.

Green, Floride. *Some Personal Recollections of Lillie Hitchcock Coit*, Grabhorn Press, San Francisco, 1935.

Hanson, W. W. *Archeology of the Cable Car*, Socio Technical Books, Pasadena, Calif., 1970.

Harte, Bret. *Gabriel Conroy*, Vols. I and II, Fields, Osgood, & Co., 1871.

Heritage House (Ladies Protection and Relief Society). Unpublished minutes, 1929-37.

Hulstad's Directories, Berkeley Section, 1908-1930.

Hunt, Dr. Rockwell Dennis. *California's Stately Hall of Fame*, College of the Pacific, Stockton, Calif., 1950.

Hutchinson, W. H. *California: Two Centuries of Man, Land, and Growth in the Golden State*, American West, 1969.

Jones, J. J. *History of the United States*, Vols. III and IV, 1902.

Kahn, Edgar M. *Cable Car Days in San Francisco*, Stanford University Press, 1940.

King, Joseph L. *History of the San Francisco Stock Exchange Board*, 1910.

Klussmann, Friedel. Unpublished personal papers.

Lavender, David. *Nothing Seemed Impossible: Ralston and Early San Francisco*, American West, 1975.

Lewis, Oscar and Hall, Caroll D. *Bonanza Inn*, Alfred A. Knopf, 1939.

Lloyd, B. E. *Lights and Shades of San Francisco*, A. L. Bancroft, San Francisco, 1876.

Lyman, George D. *Saga of the Comstock Lode*, Charles Scribner's Sons, 1937.

———. *Ralston's Ring*, Charles Scribner's Sons, 1937.

Manchester, William. *The Glory and The Dream: A Narrative History of America*, Little, Brown & Co., 1973.

Menefee, C. A. *Sketch Book of Napa, Sonoma, and Mendocino*, Napa City Reporter Publishing House, 1873.

Mitchell, Ruth Comfort. *Old San Francisco*, D. Appleton Century Co., Inc., 1933.

Muscatine, Doris. *A Cook's Tour of San Francisco*, Charles Scribner's Sons, 1969.

———. *Old San Francisco: The Biography of a City from Early Days to the Earthquake*, G. P. Putnam's Sons, 1975.

Neville, Amelia Ransome. *Fantastic City*, Houghton Mifflin, 1932.

Olmstead, Roger and Watkins, T. H. *Here Today*, Chronicle Books, 1968.

San Francisco Great Register 1872, A. L. Bancroft Publisher.

Shuck, Oscar. *Bay of San Francisco*, 1892.

Shumate, Albert. *The California of George Gordon*, Arthur R. Clark, 1976.

Stevenson, Robert Louis. *Silverado Squatters*, Chatto & Windus, London, 1883.

———. *Vailima*, Chatto & Windus, London, 1883.

Stoddard, Charles Warren. *In The Footprints of the Padres*.

Wells, Evelyn. *Champagne Days of San Francisco*, Doubleday, 1947.

Williams, Bruce Charles. Article on Enrico Caruso, *San Francisco Magazine*, April, 1967.

Wilson, Carol Green. *History of the Heritage House: 1853-1970*, Lawton & Alfred Kennedy.

Joyce Jansen moved to San Francisco from Minneapolis in 1946. She has spent years in the world of books, both in promotion and as a literary agent. She has also worked in public relations for the Sheraton-Palace Hotel, the Mark Hopkins Hotel, and the San Francisco Municipal Railway. Joyce achieved official cable car buff status in 1961, when she worked with Friedel Klussmann to organize the celebration of Muni's fiftieth birthday.

Woodford Press, a division of
Woodford Publishing, Inc.
660 Market Street, Suite 206
San Francisco, California 94104
(415) 397-1853

Laurence J. Hyman, *Publisher and Creative Director*
Kate Hanley, *Editor*
Jim Santore, *Art Director*
David Lilienstein, *Marketing Director*
Tony Khing, *Advertising Director*
Paul Durham, *Marketing Assistant*
Debbie Fong, Heather Torain, *Editorial Assistants*